CW00428594

Introduction

"Middle class boy ventures to India, becomes traumatised by the country's poverty, escapes its reality through drugs, then gradually assimilates the experience, emerging changed. A reflective account on the journey of a lifetime."

This journey began in 1990 when I was 18 and had recently left school. A younger man than me speaks through this book – views held then and now have altered – I have stayed faithful to my original writings undertaken after my return.

Except my own, names have mostly been changed in case anyone minded.

Any financial profit I make from this will be given to a mental health charity near where I live.

The cover picture is the one I created in hospital.

Is This Me   1995

Confidently arrogant
Very self assured
Nothing is too difficult
Impossible to be bored
Ever free and easy going
Worldly wise and all-knowing
Well travelled and experienced
Naive, innocent, easily led
Into the ever next adventure real
No hesitation or questioning
Forwards on with boundless zeal
Just full-on living, being, real.

Chapter 1

A hurried departure, rush to the car and fast drive to the airport at Heathrow to make the plane. Bags already packed, we only had to throw them in. We did not have breakfast as Martin, my school friend travelling companion with the tickets, forgot about getting to the airport an hour beforehand and so we were rushing and I was panicking in case we actually missed the plane. As it was, we arrived three quarters of an hour before it left, not that it seemed to matter in the exciting atmosphere of our epic journey about to commence. Martin and I boarded the plane, he, unusually, showing more calm at this departure than me.

Stop-off in Abu Dhabi. Stepping out the plane was a shock-blast of air, of heat and slowness never before experienced. The small, quiet airport, white buildings, modern conveniences; no point in leaving the airport as it was only an hour or two until the collecting plane picked us up. I found out then that we were not permitted to leave the airport during our visit. This knowledge, coupled with the numerous automatic-weapon-wielding policemen, was uncomfortable. Perhaps almost as much as the heavy twelve hole boots the police wore, clearly of gross discomfort in this hot clime. We friends conversed, ate a bit and amused ourselves, boredom before boarding. I broke into some crossword puzzle books my younger sister had given me, I was touched by the thoughtfulness of the gift, a great thing to keep my mind working in a familiar way in an unfamiliar setting.

Sunset below the clouds on the horizon. No camera was my first thought, really the sight was so unusual and exciting that I wished I could have shared it with people, but I had to enjoy it for what it was in the moment. A fleeting image out of the window, high in the atmosphere, a taste of wonder, the plane flew above the clouds into the night. It made the modern, uncomfortable, noisy, polluting aeroplane flight okay for a little while, allowing us to see the sun and the clouds in a way such as this. As the plane tore through the sky in its noisy way, I felt overcome by this breathtaking sight. I remember this image as a taste of what was to come; after seeing this, the journey felt right, with Martin by my side.

Small, dense light clusters were visible from my window, a shock of mysticism, the earthiness of the intricate dwellings seemed so very eastern, this ambience being perceived from the heights, at night. It was a suprise that I could sense this place so far below, the feeling wafting upwards was of a city or town where there was a concentration of people. I thought they might hear the plane overhead and mind at the noise, but instead what I felt was not disapproval but a peace from the people below that I unexpectedly fell into as well.

Chapter 2

On arrival, we walked through to the airport exit, the musty slowness and thickness of the air at once surrounding us, as did the peaceful atmosphere. The expensive bus took us past miles of slums, miles of unimaginable hardship, the unforgettable smell reaching out to us. The calm, dark, early Bombay morning was penetrated by blots of light and the noisy speeding bus ripping past the thousands upon thousands of desperate people. How were there so many of them? How could things be so bad? Why were they all here? Oh my God! Part of me shut off from it all, there was no way I could even process it. After a long while, the slum gradually changed into buildings, the smell, the suffering and the horror reduced but, already, it was etched into my memory.

They are always expensive, the buses that wait to take you somewhere when you arrive in nowhere on scheduled transportation and you have to get elsewhere. The sort of money that we gave to the driver would have fed a whole slum family for a week, I later found out the extent of extortion when I spoke with a German on the bus.

In Bombay we walked, wandered about a bit, feeling tired but elated, declined numerous offers to buy hashish. We passed a man without legs in a small cart pushing himself along and a white BMW drove down the road beside him. Headed for the Lonely Planet-recommended traveller digs area, I photographed the harbour at dawn, near the Gateway to India. We walked to different places, trying to do so without the persistent offer of help by a self-appointed guide; we accepted him after much plod, he showed us a couple more places and sorted us out. We gave rupees, tipping him for finding us a good place at a good price.

Dumped stuff, locked room, used own padlock, went strolling, loaded with rupees. Came back, slept a bit, headed out again to the bustling chaos, found a market area that evening and bought sandals. Off came the trainers there and then and not once did I put them back on. The sandals cost about thirty pence and were made beautifully. We wandered along a bit and found a little stall serving fresh cooked food, we dared and ate, it looked good, but boy was it hot! Mouths burning, grinning - or grimacing - we were enjoying this challenge. Indian herbal heat in our mouths, amused stall holders, such boldness. A stiff lesson, this is how the food will be.

Returning to our room together, we rested. I lent my comic to the guy next door, we met him in the hall, a German who shared some grass with us. We had met him on the airport bus, then again here, he said he'd bought it off a kid who offered him the lowest price, he had checked with all the pedlars. We giggled until the comic returned, Martin pointing out that waiting for its return was delaying us settling down. I laughed so much at this that I fell off the bed, the Furry Freak Brothers had delayed our sleep, stoned on the first night.

It was a nice room to stay in, the tacky market stalls crowding outside making the pavement less wide, even a Lonely Planet guide for sale. The street activity of stalls and selling meant immediate bombardment upon exiting the hotel. We visited the Gateway to India again, tourists, no I do not want postcards, no peace and quiet. We left for Bangalore that next morning, the chaos overwhelmed us.

Chapter 3

Mammoth train journey, twenty four hours. We paid our seat reservers handsomely at Bombay, the guides having shown us the right train and found some seats, sitting on them while we stored the bags above. Two rupees given to someone clever, they must have walked away smiling, though it was a city and the money would not have lasted long. After the seat transaction, I watched. On the platform, a hand wagon was being loaded, the huge heavy pile briefly weighted so that the guy on the frontward handles was temporarily airlifted, while trying to hold it down, the busy young men laughed.

A mother, two small kids, opposite us, dirty sari and one ill, silent. Martin gingerly handed purified water, creating awkwardness. I thought he'd cracked a bit, I thought our water was the wrong thing to offer entirely. It must have been best they were left to get on with it. We hijacked the luggage rack to act as a bag rest, a bed and watch position. We swapped our sleeping position, taking turns between the luggage rack utilised as a bed and a thin space on the seat, always keeping an eye on the stuff. Much to see from the windows, cramped and dark inside.

The slow train ground onwards, we bought a bite at the stations now and then, one piece tasted awful, felt ashamed to waste it, I got a smile from a chap near me. Martin's guitar playing in the dark train's interior, outside it seemed like another world. I couldn't believe he was playing, felt really embarrassed but got into it, people liked it for a while. Later someone came along singing music when the train stopped. Martin afterwards got out his guitar again and played, trying to imitate the charmingly repetitive tune. Glad he did not think to do that while the person was singing.

I taught and played Chinese Chequers with a business man, we spoke little, I took photos of our compartment, crowds in and out, seat, benches, floor, racks full. Martin got surprisingly friendly with the 'untouchables' on the way to the loo where they sat in the smell. I didn't happen to go while they were there, he though, shook their stumpy leprosy hands. A man from the north, sharp pointed nose, black moustache, turban wearing, tall, slim, sat near. He was not so small and cuddly as the other Indians around us, I was tall, Martin was giant-like! I saw a slum on a stop, still, watching the organic reality, a man shitting, bum to us on the tracks nearby, I took a slum building snap and a lasting look at this way of life.

Sometimes the train would stop. During the day, the lack of wind heated us all up, relief came when the breeze returned as the train started. At night, I would wake, wondering why we had stopped, falling back to sleep once the movement resumed, a sense of reassurance that we were again on our way.

Twenty four hours on from Bombay station, the journey done second class, we walked towards the bus station from the Bangalore train, avoiding the seemingly hundreds of motor rickshaws queued up and waiting to fleece tourists and travellers. We took one which was a bit further away from the crush outside of the station square, to get out of that might itself have cost too much! Could have taken a bus I suppose but this new way of travel was fun and the driver knew where the bus station was.

We got our tickets and had time to spare before the bus came, a most odd wait in the hospital gardens, near the bus station. An old lady selling peanuts was friendly to us, woven wicker basket on head, haggish smile, even giving us them free on top of the plenty we bought. She ate them too so they must have been good. We sat and relaxed, looked at the flowers, we had an hour. I chatted with a doctor and made a potential pen friend, on the way to the loo in the hospital. He was up against a lot, being stationed in India, I told him that there were many Indian doctors in England.

After my stroll, we sat on a bench and were slowly surrounded by ten, then thirty, then fifty people. The crowd looked on while we sat doing nothing, they did nothing too. I was perhaps, a pony tailed, acne spot on forehead, breastless, bearded woman, the spot sitting between and just above the eyebrows like a bindi. My tall, blonde, curly haired friend entertained with the guitar after being driven mad by the staring, standing crowd. I found the pressure intimidating, moving away to take a photo of the enormity of the gathering around us two rather normal people. I was a bit freaked out that they could be so bored.

Chapter 4

A manically bumpy and packed bus to Silpurham, Martin standing surf-style at the back of the bus. Total chaos all around, in contrast to the constant route we took. We were tired when we arrived, walking into the peaceful surround, a stillness - although anything would have been after that bus ride. Wearily we walked the long way to our ashram destination, past Christian graves looking most out of place.

We arrived and saw a job in hand, I chucked down my bag and watched. Standing atop a branchless, tall tree, having climbed barefooted, was a man sawing and throwing, so the wood could fall away from the house below. I quickly volunteered to climb way-up and heaved on the saw. Death was the fall, off were my sandals, hands on the handle, up there high, giving more of a view to the blue, blue sky and surround. He was further up, I had climbed below, two hands on the bow saw. I said to him, get higher up so he could push from above and I could pull from below. He was scared, so I did the climbing, still further up, with him below, very nervous I was, but okay when concentrating on sawing through the trunk. The other chap stayed up, after I came down, he carried on when I had enough, sweating, trembling with nerves. I did just this little bit but he carried on far longer before climbing down. Trunk sawn to pieces then pulled down with a rope to keep from falling on houses. Branches, falling free, hacked apart after landing. Firewood was this now dead tree to be, too tall to fell with one cut at the base. I was pleased that I'd done such a feat, a hero within the community straight away, I'd say!

Leaving the team to the task at hand, many people standing around, we were shown into the main house; no Amelia, Martin's friend whom we'd been rather hoping to meet. We watered and shortly were shown our lodgings at the nursery school digs where we popped our bags in the playgroup room. Not the safest place so we left them under padlock, we packed away each day, children were not using it during our stay but something of Martin's, he said, got taken away, a little money it was, oh well.

Our lodgings were a smart place, a beautiful one, we agreed, the gardens of fruit-laden trees, a bushy tree-lined path, leading down from the steps, flowers of colour, trimmed hedges. Peace, away from the central ashram spot. We lay on the floor, I crashed out, I think I didn't give a shit, I was so tired after the long, long journey.

This Christian ashram, in a Hindi / Muslim surround, a special place, though surely not an Eden. I believed that not everything could be sound in this island of Christianity.

Chapter 5

Real integration soon began, we were here to work at the ashram, today off first, then our contribution could start. The deep sleep recharged, then lunch, and Amelia was there. Not quite the stunner I'd hoped for, but never mind, she was very nice and gay. She stayed a little walk away with other girls, a long term stay, long dark brown hair, big expressive eyes, nice wide smile, tall, strong, and really into being there which I thought a little square. Not in a wild atmosphere these people, not at all, but restful, and Amelia liked that. She'd been in town, I think, when we'd arrived.

Now a sitting down Indian style meal, first passing through the beavering, busy feminine atmosphere cooking kitchen place. We were led to a mat on the floor, the dining room area, sitting, chatting, and saying hello. All food shared was the motto at communal meals. Most folk attended, teachers from the school, people in the main house and guest area, no villagers. This sharing regime was, I found, a little strained, as food got cold before tucking in. So many dishes being politely passed around so many people, making sure that every person got a chance to have something of everything. It must have been a Christian rule, so I obeyed, nervously eating, being as polite as possible, imitating some of the Indian manner. The sharing spirituality appealed to me, that the nice spread of cooked food could be enjoyed in such a mood, amidst a great deal of harmony.

A few things to say on the day to day ashram scene. Alison, the head woman, gave us our initial introduction and our job, fencing, was announced, followed by quite quiet conversing about our trip in a polite, constrained kind of way. Should I finish the bowl or is that piggish? I ate confidently and quite well, Martin did too, our appetite was large, I felt okay that we both did not eat the most, although Martin had more than me. I do not think our hosts thought us greedy, it was just what I thought of, and on subsequent meals I concentrated on not finishing the serving bowls off. There were two or three Indian kitchen serfs, Amelia, two other young Indian girls, one looked older, a potter. The English-ish lady Alison, she would keep going off, changing the mood, to attend to her kids, two young ones, a buggy nearby. She was wife to the man of the ashram, an English man, the leader who was away on a trip.

After the meal, Alison came through the back door of her house, white clothed, we were shown the shower area, just near the ladies' garden, next to a big shed place. I later made my way to the enclosed shower space, stone floored area, bucket of water and the gutter to hand, a douse, so fresh, no soap. Feeling rejuvenated, I dried vaguely, knowing the weather would soon do the rest for me. I had never stood naked for so long under the sun; without a roof on the cubic space, I could almost feel I was outside. I changed and strolled to see more of the ashram area.

This consisted of our nursery place, a school, the main house adjoining the communal kitchen / eating area. Away a little distance, the ashram building, centre of art production, it was a Christian art ashram. The two German girls had a house, near to the gardener's house, a friendly man; a bit off the beaten track lived Amelia and the two Indian girls. Further away still from the central eating area was the village, here lived Indians, some working at the school and nursery. Here too were shops, selling beedies, land workers' houses, farmers, clay brick makers and a church in the village where we went once.

We went to see the art ashram hall, a circular corrugated iron roofed place, compacted mud floors, spacious, empty. I went with Martin, who had been told the way, and I met Lordu there, a shy wood carver, lovely chap. He said to pop in, and soon became my friend. Abiding near the confines of the circular built hall, he'd come to study carving; he came from Kerala, English good, didn't smoke, felt embarrassed when asked. Next day, he showed us some pieces he had made in wood, seriously into that, offered us after we had seen some stuff to make something just for us, the wood cost a lot and labour was very cheap. Martin asked for something in some cheap wood, a lady, busty with snaky hair, his idea. For me, in proper carving wood, I wanted something to keep, a closed eyes Buddha head, Lordu's idea, he'd done them before so we said yes, a deal was struck. His room was small, a bed and floating in a bucket of water, wood carving block pieces; he was a small, wiry chap, black hair, moustache, dark eyes, quite serious. I really thought he knew his wood, he said we could come back to visit at his room anytime.

That was all the art there was going on, we wandered back along a path, near the village and graveyard, a slow scene, dusty path, some mud houses with poor people. Then back into the more familiar scene of recognised people, feeling calm, collected, cool, in my sandals and shorts, t-shirt and ponytail, it was hot. Strolled around the compound, they cook with methane gas in the kitchen from human shit-filled pits, very environmental this. A Christian community, everything going swell, people in native dress, saris, lungis (a fold-up sort of male-worn skirt), smiles, all was going well.

Supper was tasty, like lunch it came with a dodgy, awful Christian prayer beginning before serving. Again we had to wait until all food was on our plates, a mix up of arms as the main bowls were passed around, then at last the long wait ended and we could eat. I ate not too much this time, but my crossed legs would not remain crossed, the barefooted, floor-seated mat-table ritual newness distracted my body from this difficult positional readjustment. A bigger seated crowd than lunch, after the meal we introduced ourselves, rotating to all around the mat, what better way to forget names, but as usual Martin needed only to be told once, then I knew I could ask him whenever I wanted.

We were keen though to do our job, entrusted with fencing a

fruit garden area with barbed wire, to stop people taking short cuts through it. It's only fair we agreed, this was a good way to earn our keep, had a look that evening with Martin, no worries, we were keen, thought we would get it all done in a week! A good meal, some quiet time, then, thankfully, to sleep.

Chapter 6

The next morning, in our cotton sleeping bag liners, no bag, we awoke to sun, breakfasted with sandals, shorts and t-shirt, nearly crosslegged again on the floor. Shown by Alison, the granite, thin, long posts, between which the thorny wire was to be brought, quite long it was, we made a start as the day drew hotter. The wire we stretched between the stones, we were soon left on our own. Hot sun beat down, we pulled the wire and frowned, getting red and heat sore in the head. Rest midday, work, no way! After a bit of twisting the wire by hand to loop around the posts then tugging it all with bare hands, we'd got up a few strands, three thick was the idea, and it was just not fun. With sore hands, we ate lunch back at the house, no cutlery was supplied, except to serve from the bigger bowls onto our plates.

I was in a miserable state about our task which, in the midday sun, was slow, with hands, doubly so, but Martin's willpower won, so we continued after eating. And we made it fun. I'd seen wire more taut than this, I thought, but at least the job was getting done, cutting the un-barbed bits of wire with the fencing pliers. We heaved and tugged and strained and looped, the fence growing, the heat, us slowing, very few posts done. The grass, fruit trees, and the occasional breeze, from the plain-like outer surround where there were more people, but we, us two, were alone with this wire and these posts, we would sit, rest and chat, squint. When we went from the fence it was only to have a pee someplace. Water in bottles, we took and drank there, the stuff from the ground which everyone else drank is what we had too, no puritab used.

On returning to the ashram, the sun and shadows were longer, ourselves smiling internally after a good job and feeling relaxed. I sat down on the steps outside of our playgroup patch, looking along the path, green square hedge with pink flowers scattered, stony path and lowering sun, no wind, or clouds, bright blue overhead, relaxed at last. Then, argh! Martin's guitar. I'd heard some of those tunes before, already, I hoped he didn't mind my taking audience outside. A little restful lie down seemed a good idea, the guitar was about the only noise that I could hear, please Martin, when I lie down inside, play it outside of here, or stop. I rested my head and he, Martin, wrote, a diary he started keeping up, reading a book too. On my white cotton lining I lay, thinking through what had happened that day. We were a little sunburnt and really tired from the sun's constant presence, physically fit we both were, but that heat which we were unaccustomed to, drained us.

Supper soon came and I started being more bold about tucking in, as were some of the women who worked in the kitchen area, I had noticed. The discomfort soon left when scooping straight in. I was beginning to master the cutlery of the hands, scooping with JCB three finger digger-like motion, then pushing with thumb, nail slide, the sticky with sauce stuff, lumpy rice straight in the mouth as a soft lump. The washing was done, again by women in the kitchen, all the equipment passed round and piled up. The women in the house did that time consuming task for the meals three times daily, served in the main building. The unrigid rule was leave when and not before the eating had finished, though sometimes people did not stay from serving to clearing. Martin and myself were late once, everyone was seated, waiting, so we made sure for that not to happen again. I felt sometimes very hungry, but usually restricted my appetite as was polite. Martin started on his secret nursery stored supply of food and sweets, I, contented, had none.

Around the meal mat, matters of everydayness were discussed, the ashram artist leaderman, Kalle with his grey beard had arrived back, seemingly important, busy and knowing looking. Some banter went on with me and the two German girls who had been there six months. I asked Alison if there was a recorder which I might blow, there was, great! The next day it was dug out of her house and lent. The child of the ashram leader was being a bit stubborn tonight and dealings by the mother were done, an embarrassment felt by me at such triviality, that it could disturb the smoothness of the resting meal. Village Indians, I felt, had much greater problems than a child causing grief. And so, the days on the fence continued, the midday rest period was agreed between us and the sun, thus we worked in this way to get more done.

Chapter 7

After a couple of days, we toured the school in the morning, Amelia was helping there and it was in full swing, the children sitting, singing, a beautiful sound to have around. They all sat together, I wanted to join in, to teach, I hardly sing but can hum a bit to an easy tune. This is not my thing, not as much as fencing, I couldn't more than half-heartedly join in and the urge to help there soon disappeared, just too much newness. The life and energy were exciting, the songs a touch regimented, we saw school no more but pressed on with our task. They had their routine, that I could not be part of, or get into. I thought, no, I was here to drift, without all the basics that come with routine. I was here to ditch that habit, I felt I could live completely without structure, to strive toward that meant school was out.

Martin took a liking to the two German girls, I vaguely fancied one, and he did too, the same girl, but I was not bothered much. He and I went over to their patch, they lived together in a house, did meals there sometimes. The fanciful one wore a sari and sandals, the other more t-shirt and shorts type dress, they were due to leave soon, to tour a little bit, then return to Germany. To hear their German speaking was fun, but a touch too much different sounding, I had already been over exposed to new sounds.

Hardcore helpers they were, the sari dressed girl won my respect for her adoption of Indian dress and custom, I too was gradually adopting more Indian ways. Amelia, had immersed herself, she had cracked, thick, leathery soled feet and a sari, everyone else but us wore Indian gear it seemed. The Indian dressed German girl was like me, I could see, she was wanting to make the effort to fit in, leaving the Germanness elsewhere, and merging with what was in her immediate environment. She looked good, she had keen dress sense. Looking like she did would have pleased many Indians, winning more of their respect because of her regard for their environment which she was in at that time. I scoffed a touch at the other German for not giving over to the more enlightened eastern ways, I thought of her as being unaccepting of India, however, she helped, balancing out any disrespect generated.

I chatted with the gardener who invited us, with gesture alone.

It is amazing what you can say. Just the tuning into each other with extra sensory perception is the hard bit, but that was here, the somewhat crippled gardener, a big strong man. I saw inside his home and was amazed, a bed, a room, kitchen bit and simple simple everything. The shrine at the head of the bed, relatively expensive Ganesh, elephant God, with offerings around it, this was far more lavish than the rest of his place. We shook hands, he smiled and I left, and would acknowledge him 'namaste' (hello) each time we met thereafter, never again going into his home, he never joined us at meals. Praying hands position and nodding, said in a calm and totally peaceful way, relaxed, 'namaste', like saying 'I love you'. Through the gardens in stillness we walked, smiling at people, two young friendly Indian girls were nice, I fancied one a bit, she was young but looked so mature.

Calm and serene in the peaceful surround in the evenings, I'd play recorder to the world. The setting sun, my tunes from England, on the nursery steps, looking out for ages on my own, trying to slow down, to be in the tone of the surroundings. I'd figure out quite complex stuff and play, long hours spent, slow soothing, healing, wounds, I'm learning meditation with my tunes, I repeat the tunes and they grow. I think no-one can hear me, just Martin now and then, if an audience appeared I was quickly embarrassed and stopped even after many days of playing. Once the attractive Indian girl walked by and asked that I should not stop, and continued on her way. Martin and guitar, if on hand, helped me to breathe music out, but Martin's musical method was too organised for me.

I remembered many tunes wandering a little into improvisation. Pentangle folk music and Baroque tunes, old, improvising around them, practising with different patterns to my school oboe lessons training. I was finding a way to play soothingly, building on the tunes I knew from my musical schooling and exposure to centuries-old music too. The regular fruit trees, flowered hedging, flat grass and trees, lazy slow long sunset evenings, turning into cloudless silvery nights.

One of these nights, I was walking towards the ashram in the unlit countryside, under the star filled sky and a shooting star streaked through the heavens for several seconds, in a long, slow, straight line, exactly in the direction I was heading.

Chapter 8

I had an idea with the fence, our hands were hurting from pulling on barbed wire, the fencing tool we had was not very good. I made a new tool for us, to help, we could cut the wire okay, but when stringing it around the posts, to keep it taut, hands hurt. I had a simple Swiss Army knife given by a friend at home in London which did good service in India where it was eventually left. It sawed and cut a piece of wood, used for tensioning the wire, after experimenting, this was better than the fencing tool. Now the job was professionally done, the thorny wire was hooked on, piling on the tension, taut wire. The stick to use was taken from a woodpile and I left it near the fence that night, on returning to look for it the next day, it had gone and after asking about it, I made another one.

The wood scavenging was intense, the branches of trees were lopped off with long extended handled cutting blades, leaving bare tree trunks, top heavy with leaves, and green wood for burning. We saw a woman with a baby strapped on and a man, the husband, sawing slowly, reaching high from the ground. The trees, they were suffering, all the branches lower than this had already been removed. Another time two women did it, we saw, one cutting, one gathering, silently we watched them. They chose the few branches the trees had within extended reach. Surely this could not continue much longer as even the floor of the forest had been scavenged for everything to burn.

My carving of the bark off the fencing stick was very much different to Lordu's work. I visited him again one day and watched as he chipped at Martin's wood, he clouted with raised mallet hitting chisel, held between his feet, his longi tight around him as he sat. I took a photo or two, one close-up of the craftsman at work, he'd get the wood soon and start on my Buddha head. I thought Martin rather superior asking him to do complicated bits, the hair on my Buddha head was to be all-over, in a simpler way. I hung around, pleased to speak in English with this 21 year old man, whose family were far off. I smoked a beedie, naughty of me, I know, and sat and relaxed alone with him in a sheltered outer area. The evening wore on and he said he must go, slowly back I strolled, wondering just how long I'd delayed Lordu from doing what he may have wanted to do. He was so very welcoming, despite me hardly knowing him, as he let me into his home. I think he may have been lonely but that's a shame because he was a good gentle man. I came back another day after he said he had my wood and watched the creation of a Buddha head held between the feet, arm raised, hammer thumping the chisel, so quick and perfect.

One night I heard beats drumming in the distance, I headed towards it, past Lordu's place, he woke. We went together, I smoke beedies, he's beside me and says the villagers celebrate a death. We went on quite far, then turned back, the loudness of the drums didn't diminish. Really in tune with the throb now, I wanted to be there and look around, to feel the rhythm closer, though it remained far. Reluctantly I returned, with me and the funeral that was that, the sound, so loud I think we were still miles away on turning round, such soulful midnight ritual, a mystery heard but not seen.

Chapter 9

Now acclimatised, evening meal sittings feeling more civilized, not as painful as they once were, sitting crossed legged was uncomfortable though only slightly less so after week. My weak knees dislocation feeling type of thing was lesser, soft ankle bones hardening, experimenting with one leg crossed at a time. The ashram man Kalle had thick skin on the sticking out bits of his ankles from so much of this sitting.

I heard a supper story, a man who lived ninety years and takes a berry and herb brew. He lives till one hundred and thirty, then takes another mix as he's lying in bed, not much up to tricks, lives to one hundred and fifty. They seemed to believe this tale, what could I achieve with this inspiration? A load of crap it was really, there were some difficult names in the story, weird. They read the book, we passed it round, I took a look, my moment arrived, I read right and left with my eyes, the sermon carried on, I'd prefer a song. I read as much as the person before, some folk read quite a lot, I gave it just a quick shot. We sat around the large mat, nothing supporting backs, passed the bowls, ate by hand, everyone speaks English, I could understand.

I spoke with two Indian girls, the short potter was not there much, I didn't see much of her pottery either, even after Amelia had discussed the idea with her of me visiting her workshop in Bangalore.

One was middle class, I favoured her, with pure smooth skin, tall, intelligent, beautiful. She had a father who made big changes, a revolutionist, speaking with farmers, persuading them to give back land, to share, with people, with the lower hands, the workers, empowering them with ownership and responsibility.

Alison, the lady of the ashram, was an English woman, seemed she had emigrated to India. With hair tied back, simple clothes, brown wrinkled skin, bare feet like an aged westerner she was someone who seemed stressed, whose mood didn't match the relaxed others. Kalle, her husband man with the master plan, he had built the art ashram. I could not see the art flowing, the creative process and inspiration, completed works of art in a gallery were nowhere to be seen. I had expected there to be many busy painters working hard together to create a grand amount of work each day, but there just seemed to be Lordu.

The German girls that taught at the school were going home soon. The pretty glasses wearing, long straight brown haired sari wearer, Martin kissed and snogged in the ashram room. The wood carver Lordu peeked at them, he'd been trying for ages to get her attention. Lordu spoke with Martin at length about relationships between young couples in India, how courtship is something that lasts, that things develop slowly, how it is a subtle process and a beautiful one. Although apparently he had asked one of the Germans for sex, perhaps thinking the western courtship rules different.

We saw them again after they had left, the pretty one got ill, they were in a Bangalore hotel, their travelling delayed, their leisure tour halted after their ashram work. We had fun finding where they were staying, bumpy rickshawing. An hour or two we stayed, played cards, went on our way.

A man with a wife and kids visited the ashram, a brother of someone on television, I recognised a likeness. He painted a rock and some other landscapes, feeling enthused, he had travelled far to view the rock from different angles. He gave a talk, showing us the paintings and describing how he saw things in the rock, it was nice to know this was going on at the ashram.

The meals were an array of stainless steel beakers and bowls, one was passed, dished out and passed on. I liked the way you always got passed food. It was standard stuff, rice, vegetables, various dishes, not too spicy, healthy and wholesome. I dug straight in after my few days of hesitance and following the cordiality of not eating until everyone had their share. After these few days I didn't care, I wanted it while it was hot, Martin's' looks! It eased the tension for me, the digging in, some Indian others ate early and heartily as I did, the ones who had been in the kitchen preparing.

Another weird evening story: meditation on hilltops, a man able to move clouds through the power of his mind. I thought the fact the clouds were moving in tune with the persons' desires meant that he was in harmony with the movement of the water vapour. Clearly, actually being able to move clouds with the power of your mind was impossible. Enthusiastic discussion by the males but not me. The story was played on a battered tape recorder machine and Kalle was not in the least bit harmonious with it, struggling to use the equipment, funny to me.

Chapter 10

There was a trip into Bangalore, we bussed in, aiming for the market, I took some time out alone in order to meet up later. Sat in a cafe with pictures for sale on the walls, looking at them for a long time, a sitting man with a pipe, the smoke very clearly exhaled, was the one I most liked. Civilised, very bright place inside, the pictures really were fine, wanted to buy one, but declined for the logistical difficulties of getting it back home again.

I took a bus trip somewhere and the bus broke down, everyone off, no refunds (we need it to repair the bus), the pavement filled up with ex-passengers. Amid the chaos as I stood aloof and wondering what to do and where I was and which direction I should go, I was in no hurry, a friendly guy started chatting to me. He spoke good English and made conversation, I walked with him and met his friend, they were students and they really wanted to give me a tour of Bangalore. I assured them I had not been here before and welcomed them to show me around.

We had a chai and talked some more, they were doing a long course in Bangalore at the university, and were on a day off from it today. They paid the chai and off we went to Victoria Gardens in a rickshaw, I knew that I was not going to be ripped off, as the Indians were sure to be able to negotiate between themselves for a low fare. My western appearance was one that implied that I would have a lot of money in my possession, though I travelled that day with very little, except one big note for emergencies. I felt safe with them as my guides, we stepped off and entered the park, I paid for a third or so of the fare and we were even. The gardens were well kept and a pleasure to stroll in, we walked and talked. I had a lot of questions about being a uni student. I was hoping myself to become one when I returned to England; having been accepted onto an engineering course, I could just about consider myself an engineering student. One guy was on a work related course in the chemistry area and the other in English or something.

We sat on a bench under some trees, them blowing in the light wind, and exchanged excitedly our views of the world, I decided that I did not want an ice cream from the tourist stall. We walked on to the high part of the park, the rocks jutting up higher than the trees. Strolling up, it afforded a spectacular view of the whole of Bangalore, houses, offices, roofs in all directions, a sea of squarish human houses. I took a photo of the three of us, utilising for the first time the delayed shutter response timer, giving me enough time to run around and be in the photograph with them, putting my arm around one of them.

We went back to their digs, there they fed me, by now I was becoming embarrassed to the extent that this hospitality had gone and refused a meal in my mind, but verbally accepted it. I met a friend or two of theirs and studied briefly some pages of a textbook, written in English in exceedingly heavy language that quickly bored me to tears, how did they enjoy that I wondered. The book was like some of the older library versions of the school science textbooks, written in the 1950s when science was the rage and nobody knew very much when they thought they knew just about everything. I chatted with one of them in depth as he spoke much clearer English and was less tiring to communicate with than the others. I eventually left them, walking out of the shady, cool flat, amid their friends whom I had been introduced to. These old fashioned courses were not for everyone, these people seemed all to be fairly affluent, but at least they were choosing to be educated, and were really lovely.

I met up with the ashram others again at the very bustling, large Bangalore market. Amelia was buying a present before leaving, a tea maker or coffee strainer thing, the other was in bad repair. The market was immense and chock-full of stalls, fruit, vegetables, spices on plates in tall cones of powder that came right to the very edge. They were all different colours, incense wafting out on passing some places, it was tragically busy, famous and beautiful.

We just walked around buying the odd bit of fruit and munching, chatting and being tempted to 'come to my stall'. There were some more shop sort of places too, these seemed long standing, more wooden house-like structures than stalls. Folk may well have lived in them, crowded around their stock which was put outside on display in the daytime, stacks of pots, pans, steel cups, steel everything, shiny and new. The pots came in sizes from the small to enormous, stacks upon stacks of them outside high class looking places to the more down town, all a bit unglamorous really but I was interested to see what the Indians used to cook with in their kitchens.

The fact that there were so many stalls near to each other in this part of the stainless steel kitchen utensil part of the market must have meant that the prices between stalls did not vary much and Amelia did not bother shopping around as we hung about and looked. She choose one without much fuss, had it hand wrapped nicely in paper with the respect given to objects that is a rarer thing in the west, after all, this was a relatively expensive thing.

The stock was a fortune worth a few hundred pounds, I thought, outside of the larger stalls. So, relatively, they must have been rolling in money; it might have been a better idea to have bought from one of the smaller stalls where there was a bit less of a selection in order to help them. Here, I had a feeling that these people, being so poor would be glad of any business that came their way.

Chapter 11

One day Amelia and I took lots of children on a trip along a track, I noticed how cracked and thick her bare footed soles had become. I became really interested in this phenomenon and looked at everyone's thick skinned feet. Amelia's were really developed, her being a westerner made me keen that my feet should become so thickened, we walked along, played some games.

For a while we played, running down a shale slope, pushing people nicely, having a great laugh, I really pushed Amelia a long way down just as the game was closing, we fought our way back up and it started up again. The kids found some fruits on a tree, throwing stones to get the food down, I helped them. A little crippled kid, couldn't run, was holding onto the fruit, he was the boss boy. He shared it out at my request as he seemed a bit grabbing and had plenty, you had to peel the stuff. A farmer came and shouted at us. Once he had left we took only a little bit more fruit, a few handfuls, the fun was all stopped with the stern telling off.

On the way back I had more friendship fun with the kids, we ran very fast in a big chain, me in the middle, kids trailing either side holding hands. Along the path we went running and jumping on every bump that ran straight across. The kids thought it great fun, the little guy at the back couldn't keep up, Amelia too was running. I slowed down to wait for the little fruit hoarder man who had had his fruit picked for him.

That evening we sat and listened at Amelia's place, in the shade, to a cassette tape or two of music, a real luxury thing, the sound really stunning at first then dulling to normal. Amelia meditated, so did I, a bit, and got the gist. Looking out at the view I felt a bit left out with Martin and Amelia chatting together so I sat aside. Looking at the trees in the fading light, the grass and gardens, the peaceful ashram. It was quite hard work on the fence, yet somehow an idyllic place. I'd have done more arty stuff if there had been an active workshop or studio about, all I did was play the recorder most evenings, which I loved.

Chapter 12

There was going to be an eclipse one night, after supper. When it was darkening we got ready for the lark, not much to bring, too warm for many clothes, we walked towards Amelia's, Martin and me. He didn't bring his torch and walked in sandals, I walked in bare feet, this I was doing more frequently. Winding on the tiny thin tracks towards the white house with the moon bright, full and silver. The little house of white, seemingly remote, we settled down, chatted much. I didn't take a photo or two, did I purposely forget so I would remember it more? Amelia had this thing that she got on an intense meditation course, that you put down your nose and round through your throat out through the mouth, a massager to soothe, strange, pulling it back and forth.

The moon started getting covered, we watched for hours till fully covered it was. On concealment the girls went to bed, much time had been spent, Martin and Amelia chatted for a bit. I saw the moon so clearly, every crater, hole, nook and cranny, the starry sky too was easier to adjust to. I thought of the girls, lying below me in the house, was the pretty one thinking of me? The silver moon had taken on a new form for me, I could see the sphericality, such clarity.

Next was the reverse, a slow, revealing slip back to a shiny thing. Since, I have thought about the whereabouts of the sun to the moon in these instances. I didn't think of the sun then, just the light that I could see on the silvery moon. I slipped off for a pee or two during the evening night, down to the ground, careful of the feet. I could see my way, far from the path I did not stray, thistley plants, such silence, I headed for bed when the moon was a quarter revealed again, leaving others to stay for the whole show.

We went there again one evening for supper which they cooked, we helped, they washed up. I felt they were being motherly women and waiting on us, Amelia, the potter and the daughter of the changer man. They seemed to be a tight three, lively and self sufficient though needing someone strong to deal with the mice downstairs, their appearance causing much alarm and great unrest. The switched on intelligent beauty changer daughter was the woman of the house as far as I was concerned, she made the least hysteria over the little creatures.

Chapter 13

We went again into the town of Bangalore, in the jeep with loads of us piled in the back, the day was hot. We dropped Amelia off at the station, she had finished her ashram work, we were to meet up in a few days when we too were finished.

The little girl of the ashram owners became very upset and didn't stop crying, even when Mum bought her an ice cream. I approached the girl when we were back and talked, finding she missed Amelia now that she was gone. I thought the reason she was crying was because of one little girl about her age who came up to the back of the jeep and begged at us all in the back at a city traffic lights. We all did nothing and I watched in pity and dismay as none of us offered a thing, nor our attention. She was just standing there in the fumes with her hand held out, so beautiful and so young.

I kept on looking at the ashram girl in the back of the jeep thinking how lucky she was, she could be like the little beggar girl, and yet there she was, not seeming to appreciate her fortune. We sat in that traffic and that girl stayed behind us, desperately pleading with us, someone had to do something soon, she was dominating the whole scene and could not be ignored. I had nothing but notes to give her, so I did not give, thankfully Amelia decided to drop a bit of change into her hand. Phew – relief that the need had been met, our collective conscience in the back of the jeep now restored that we had given where it was so needed.

The jeep stayed stationary in the traffic and the girl still stayed behind us, holding out her hand, soon joined by other children of similar ages, no way was anyone going to give them all something. The traffic did not move and the bundle of children stood there pleading and holding out their hands, please move traffic and get us out of this hell, I can't bear those children. I had had a break from the begging for a week and a half and I didn't want to be reminded of it just now. Just because I had been away from the poverty-stricken towns for a while did not mean the problems had diminished, just the memory.

The traffic at last moved on, leaving the pathetic straggle of children in dirty rags, ill, exhausted, breathing in the fumes, dying more than living. The expense of the ice cream bought afterwards was comparatively great and I had refused to have one, feeling so guilty about the little girl. She was not alone in that traffic jam but it was her voice that reached deep within me, that fear in her voice, pleading with us to give her some money, though she needed so much more than that.

The beggar had made me full of turmoil about giving money to these children whose problems are just not solved by giving money; in fact, they may make them worse, as begging then becomes more widely undertaken, the more profitable it is. I had heard stories about the oppression of these desperate people, being coerced into giving all their money to intimidating bullies who become rich. The problem seems so ungovernable while there remains such huge corruption within the organisations of people who have the power to change things. Worse still is the seemingly democratic desire among people to brush such problems aside and let them get worse as they forget about them. Instead, people fulfil more immediate desires and wants for themselves, without making the extra effort to help others around them, even when they are so nearby. The root of the problem is undoubtedly overpopulation, life is so cheap because of the number of people crammed together in a crowded, polluted city, competing with each other, grinding each other into the ground, survival of the fittest, with no sort of back up social state security.

Of course projects do exist that help in a small way, but only with the acutest of problems. I feel the duty is of the people in India who are able to help, to do so as quickly and as effectively as possible. I guess this might mean that education is required to help people realise how it is they might be able to help the problems around them. I believe there are many who do want to help and who have the resources and energy to do so, but they lack courage and knowledge about how to become involved. I imagine the middle classes of India are capable of a great deal more social reform and charity work, but that it might be unfashionable to do so, and may even be looked down upon by the majority.

The thing I most believe is that the Indians themselves know best how to solve their own problems, but catalysis is needed to give a few that impetus to start to change things more, and from there a snowball effect may be expected as more and more people feel the need to help and to relieve their conscience.

Chapter 14

We left the peace of the ashram a few days later, this had been a good, gentle start to India for me in this lovely sanctuary. From Bangalore to the coast, then a boat trip sitting on the roof in the sunshine with a friendly bunch of westerners to Cochin. An eagle swept down and, as we watched it, a man grabbed his camera from his bag and took an extremely quick photo before the eagle disappeared. I thought he must have been on edge and missed the enjoyment of the moment, unlike myself who was enjoying the sun and a gentle stone, having managed to buy some in Cochin. Later on in the trip a boy ran alongside the boat shouting for 'school pen' as many children did, no one threw him a pen and he ran along for ages as we all watched. He then had to stop at a channel in the riverside, still shouting for the pen. The quick camera man reached into his bag before it was too late for the child and threw him a really good pen, the boy jumped into the water channel to retrieve it and held it above his head in victory with a big smile, much to the relief and applause of everyone on board.

The Cochin square fish nets on counterweights, up in the air in the moonlight, all quiet by the river, the place still. A little street stall with lovely smells, Kerelan fish curry with dry spicy chunks of fish with rice. One of the most enjoyable meals of my life that supper was, the perfect balance of everything, fresh fish lovingly cooked. The street stalls had been recommended as safe places to eat as you can see how things are stored and cooked so can judge the hygiene standards. We had lucked out on this one, I ate as much as I could without my stomach feeling uncomfortable.

We arrived at Kovalam after a hot bus journey, dusty busyness greeted us as we trundled off and were hassled into a taxi. It definitely couldn't fit all our bags as well as us, but somehow managed. Arrival at the beach top palms before a stroll down to the sea and general hotel area, paths down through rich, lush jungley palm forest to the bay, the shack and concrete hotels touching both the forest and the beach. A nice man got talking to us and showed us some really class handmade gear, mirrored, bright tapestries. We really did like the stuff and agreed to go to his house, but later, as we were presently very near to Amelia's parents' whereabouts. He warned us that he was to go back to his home in the country tomorrow and that this was one of the last chances we'd have to buy these bright mirror bags and bits, so we made a plan to view the stock at his house a little later on.

We found the hotel and the receptionist told us Amelia and her parents were upstairs. They were slow, gentle, into the vibe type of people; she a laid back earthy actress, he a wow-y style of talking laid back actor, done nothing there so far really, just rested and enjoyed themselves they said. Martin and I had to press on to this house as the chap was there waiting to flog his stuff, we excused ourselves from the company, left our sacks, offered them to join us and set off alone.

The mum, Sam, knew a bit, whereabouts to go and directions

were not hard to find, Martin remembering the names of where and who as he always could. Thin winding paths through to the more secluded parts behind the main drag, a late afternoon walk. Reached the house, recognised the person, and he started to haul out some things, bags for me and other nice bits for Martin. He said something about bringing them in from the country where they were made, by his family whom he supported, there was rather a lot to sell before tomorrow though. After a little deliberation I settled on a yellow mirrored bag patterned with bright leaves and animals, this I used for many years until it wore out. Martin came away with a yellow, similarly coloured blanket, we had both spent a reasonable amount but were glad that we had caught these bargains. We strolled gently back enjoying the cooling air around us, loads of westerners about, more than we'd seen before. The cool, white hotel received us again, Pete and Sam were into eating out soon which we were now more than ready for, after our long journey.

The first I'd seen of Pete and Sam was at a party in the Holland Park area of London, a block of houses enclosed a garden, friends were invited to enjoy the market, food, drink and company. I'd turned up in full Indian gear, Dad's headscarf and white cotton top and bottom, as the next appointment for me that evening had been a fancy dress party, it was fun. Sam and Pete were in the garden, Martin had introduced me, they asked about scoring some blow, it got sorted out with a chap from school, who had left the school and I'd not seen for a while. A joint was soon rolled, I'd had a smoke with them, I found out they were into relaxing and I thought they were well cool. Amelia, I thought, may have had a hard time coping with such radical, liberal parents, Sam, she was the mother, he, Pete, the boyfriend stepdad.

English food was available, the spelling on the menus was

amusing, a bizarre mixture of Indian phonetics and old fashioned English phrasing which noone seemed to have the desire to change or correct. With dark falling, the night time was just beginning, the lights were on and movement occurring, dancing drinking and naturally, smoking. But as I was keeping company with the actors, we just had a meal, a walk. I was excited at the prospect of having a smoke, but we were still getting to grips with the numerous cafes around, so it was a chat and a restful night's sleep instead.

Sun, as usual, and a late relaxed breakfast, the pace of things I quickly got into, having already slowed down to Indian restful speed, having been there now for around two and a half weeks. Eggs, toast, bread and beans, even porridge available, the expense was high as was the class of restaurant. Later, Martin got concerned enough about it for us to resort to much cheaper things on the menu, but what the heck for a few days. A leisurely breakfast, making us ready for grand things after our long sleep, there was a huge beach to walk around, the sea, things to buy, we sat in the shady cafe for quite a while.

While Martin and I strolled the beach, Pete and Sam were still around the cafe, in shade and relaxed. The sun was worshipped by a few semi-clad westerners, the Indian women all preferring to don the sari, carrying large bowls of fruit on their heads, vendors selling Thai dyed sheets, jewellery items and carvings. Later, we were set up on the beach under a palm tree in a lightly crowded area, the busier cafes and much bustle left behind. A swim in the sea had to be done, shorts, bare feet and top. Towels laid out in the sun to warm up for our wet return, well, we'd just about dried on the walk back to them, sunbathing was out. Water bottles had been bought, a few bits to eat too.

At first, the beach sellers arriving asking if we'd buy things was a disturbance, no, no, no please shoo, but some actually had really useful life-enhancing things for us to buy. Sam proved this by purchasing a large yellow melon, from one woman balancing a large straw basket on her head, loaded with colourful fruit, it was so nice, and eight rupees had to be worth it (twenty five pence at the time). Coconut oil lotion softened the skin, without frying, we got browned, the first evening me having noticeable browning marks in previously unreached places, Martin was redder than brown, neither of us really suffered. The next day we were to sort out a place to stay, having decided to hang out independently a bit, and not to intrude any more, by staying at Sam and Pete's.

Chapter 15

We went on a trip, away from the backpacker scene, on a hollowed out type of boat propelled by a fisherman who toiled away in the sun, with the added reflected sunlight from the water's surface making the going more difficult. We were going to a beach that he knew and would be picked up the next day in the morning to be taken back to Kovalam in time for lunch. He paddled us for ages, at the stern of the boat with a single vertical paddle (and no spare) we went for an hour or two. He must have become very tired but would not receive any help from me or anyone. Eventually we arrived in the wilderness, the sand was blacker here and the place pretty deserted, thank you to the boatman. The evening began to come, the temperature dropped, the scorching hot sand of the day became cold, sapping our body heat. We lit a fire with bits and pieces collected from around, feeling a little like pioneers, but knowing that it was easy going really. We warmed by the fire and cooked the fish and other bits that had been brought, it tasted all the better for the smoke of the fire.

I decided to go off for an explore and wander by myself for a bit, it was dark and to ensure that I knew my way back I headed along the beach in one direction, rather than into land. I met up with a couple of young Indian lads who were walking holding hands in that loving way that so many of the Indian men did. One of them took an interest in me, the other less so, although it might have been because his English was not as good. We walked together for a while in the night and chatted a little bit, in the silence of the uninhabited peace of the beach, the waves the noisiest thing there. They were pretty quiet and subdued, we had a smoke, I had some stuff with me, we shared a little, sitting, the three of us on the beach before soon getting up again and continuing on the way we had come.

One of the lads asked if I would like a coconut. I had taken no money and there were no shops around, so presuming that there was wishful thinking going on, I replied yes wouldn't it be great to have a bit of coconut now. We carried on walking a while and came to a line of palm trees on the upper side of the beach next to what may have been fields beyond. The quieter lad started shinning up a palm tree, I watched in amazement as he made his way to the top and threw down a coconut. It was dark and he had difficulty seeing which trees had suitable fruits to take, this meant that he climbed many trees, sometimes coming straight down again if there was no suitable bounty at the top. We soon had three coconuts, but no machete for opening them. We just peeled off the outer fibrous bit and smashed the things on rocks, with me trying to make the most of the milk inside before it poured out all over the sand. They said that some guy or other owned these trees and I realised the fact that they were stealing, but it did not bother me.

I wanted to have a go at climbing the trees, he had the knack of walking up, hugging the tree, pushing against it with his bare feet, then when the trunk became thinner slightly further up of adopting a yogic position of both soles to the trunk with knees out to the sides. I could get up five of six feet or so, up the hardest part where the tree was widest but did not have the motivation or bravery to go much higher. I began to realise when climbing the tree that I was pretty stoned, but this was great fun. Anyway, we walked back from the coconut trees, towards the camp.

The outgoing guy was chatting and we sat down on the beach for another smoke, the other guy wandered off after the smoke and two of us lay on the beach, chatting, in a slightly intimate way. The guy then suggested something and I looked down to his erect penis that he was slowly masturbating, I got the idea of what he had in mind. I thought quickly then indicated that I was not interested in him in that way. The other guy who was wandering around came over and the three of us parted company and I continued on my way, wishing them both well.

As I walked back to the camp, I thought that that was quite an experience, and I had handled it very well, not getting freaked out about it, not even talking about the sexual bit to the others. It was many weeks afterwards, as I was writing in my book, that I thought again about the incident. I had actually hesitated about saying no to the guy, I had actually seriously contemplated having sex with that Indian guy, in some way. That was what shocked me, my own sexuality being questioned, just briefly and me not being absolutely repulsed by the idea of what was on offer. I did not start thinking that I was gay, but had an open mind about this matter and a mature attitude. I had actually thought about it, he was a good looking guy, similar personality to myself in many ways, and I got on with him. He could have been a friend, quite easily, but it was not to be, just all or nothing. I slept well out in the open on the beach around the embers of the fire to wake early to a new day, and a beautifully welcoming dawn.

Chapter 16

So the days continued, the long sunny days of lounging around, bathing in sea and sun, the shady beach bars offering western music by day and night, in fact the party never seemed to stop, it just did when I did. I bought a stone carved Indian elephant from a chap who walked around to various tables, a small, well made thing except for the breakable tusks. Martin had decided to become friends with some westerners who frequented a bar to which Amelia, Sam, Pete and I went the second night. They played, or thrashed, at high speed their acoustic guitars, chord changing to make a folksy sound. Martin became captivated by playing with this crazy crowd and admitted the next morning that he had become monstrously stoned to the extent that he realised on his walk back to the hotel that he didn't know where he was, but made it home anyway. This kind of got my back up as I was the frantic party man, more so than Martin, and this reputation of mine was unquestionable.

Another evening I went along with Martin to the folksy bar, listening to the fastest strumming ever, having a chilum toke or two and becoming really head fucked on it. Martin was having increasing problems learning the chords and keeping up, but they didn't mind. I didn't bother with the guitar, there was no way I could compete, so leaving a slowing Martin, I waved cheerio after asking him if he fancied a walk to the other happening cafes that I'd noticed.

I took a walk alone along the promised land of the beachy shelters, leading me past various songs, Tracy Chapman, Doors was great to recognise. By night, other stuff had came on, a reggae place seemed good but it wasn't really for me so I pressed on and got chatting with some young English folk at tables outside a cafe. We got to playing backgammon on the tables on the sand, I had a spliff with them and got really into the backgammon, I was thinking hard, my aggressive, competitive edge taking over. I won the first, second, perhaps three of four. I played other people too and saw one person positioning their singles on safe spots where it was unlikely I'd land and be taken; these safe spots were determined by the initial pattern at the beginning. They were all friendly, a nice girl with whom I was competing had a man nearby, I left them after a bit, refusing more to smoke and turning in nicely stoned for a good heavy sleep in our nice, clean room.

Martin had found this place to stay behind a trendy club which didn't disturb us, a blue front, white balcony with view over roofs to the beach. A simple double room containing two single beds and a cupboard, the door was locked by us, the rent was ninety Rupees daily. Over subsequent days, we realised that people made that last a week in some of the out of the way downbeat places, this was of concern to us as I envisaged my money lasting me six months and Martin a bit less. It had to be budget, bargaining, tight fistedness the whole time, a high demand considering the extreme poverty everywhere, people looking very much like they were dying in front of my eyes, begging for money. This meant to me that I just couldn't starve this country of my hard won cash, accumulated by Christmas shop assistanting in a Victoria Station

London gift shop.

Chapter 17

Every day, twice, an event occurred that was so ancient that not even the topless bathers had an effect and parts of the beach were transformed. Fishing it was, and I've no doubt it is painstaking work but fascinating. The young and old fishing men from the nearby villages, haul, hand over hand, the heavy nets, pulling for their life, as they were in some ways. Far out to sea, boats put the nets into the water, swimmers are also dumped in who splash to encourage the fish towards the net and slowly swim in. On the beach, the ends of the net are hauled in a huge crescent shape, gradually becoming tighter. From the high rocks, a number of fishermen whistle to the boats, the folk above being able to discern easily the whereabouts of the shoal compared to the lower boats. The boats make their way back in, the occupants no doubt helping the tiring hauling process after the rowing out. The men on the rocks stroll down to the beach too for the hauling in. The muscles of the older men's arms are fantastic, they are of great health, its all those fish for sure. Three hours it takes, now that is a long time to tread water and splash hands for the two or three fish scarers, imagine that twice a day for a lifetime!

Pete helped the men one day, he said it was great to be part of what was happening, my feelings were a little guilty that this effort was going on while I was being a complete waster in comparison. Feeling too, I did, that I just couldn't genuinely take part with them without becoming a hindrance to the plan, I took only photos of the event and feel now that I am instead helping them by passing on this information to whoever is interested.

I thought I sort of recognised a girl from a camp in England, well she was twenty fiveish, a woman. I was running on the hot sand between umbrellas and cafes, she spotted me, on closer inspection it was her. Kat, with the clear crystal, no-one-else-touch-this necklace, it was hers only, she was a bit quiet, good looking and up for a drink. The 'what a small world' and 'I can hardly believe this, what in India!' formalities were quickly dispensed, our friendship grew, Martin liking her too. She had only just or perhaps very recently arrived in Kovalam and was looking for a room, her stuff was in a hole of a place, I think stashed with some barmy friend. We offered her that she could stay with us for a few days, which she took up. I wondered what situation she was in before at Kovalam.

Three in a two bed place worked, a delight, it was in many ways that she was so easy going. The way she fitted in so well was such that she was great, a motherly figure who was sexy too, mainly motherly. I thought she was deeply in need of healing. Sharing the hotel room, there was the problem of undressing, this sorted itself out with us all stripping off and being hopelessly unashamed of our nudity. I was glad that I had become well acquainted with one of such street credibility as Kat, she was not totally sorted but I thought of her as very cool and felt that I had made a true friend with her in my own way.

Chapter 18

We planned to go from Kovalam to a tiger sanctuary – Mundanthurai - further south in Kerala. The sanctuary was only three or so hours on the bus, so with sweat and rucksacks, together we three rode, the windy roads giving Martin fun at the front of the bus panorama, clutching the sacks dumped on the floor. It was a pleasure to have the company of cool Kat, we looked at the passing scenery, largely contented, arriving late afternoon. This was a nature park, lines of real soldier ants carrying things busily, a millipede over twenty centimetres long which crawled, bending its sections over things in its way. These delights we explored, waiting for a official to turn up, sacks on the table.

Then we heard, and soon saw at closer range, the monkeys, a very excited lot they were indeed. A bad idea to feed them it was, we were hungry and snacking, although food was promised for later, they begged in a way that made us interested in them and unaware they were after food. Martin decided to photo one, hands and feet apart, shinning along a telephone wire towards us. Then a monkey leapt cleanly onto his unguarded snack of peanuts and away at lightning speed amid great clamour among all the monkeys. Up the tree it went, frantically pursued by loads of mates, running the branches, the nuts travelled far, after a few minutes the plastic sack, only a little depleted, fell to earth from the tree. Martin picked it up, deciding they could have them anyway. The noise calmed and the monkeys made running forays to the scattered nuts on the ground, I felt a bit put out at this invasion of our privacy.

An Indian wait later, watching the scenery of the park, a chap arrived and walked with us barefooted to a concreted ugly guest house that was somewhat antsy, antsy to an unpleasant extent in fact. The back loos were antsy and the mattresses outside had a unbelievable amount of life in them we discovered, deciding they were not so good to use as a bed as hoped. So straight onto the metal springy bed bottom it was. Little used accommodation, but cool with metal iron beds, elite trippers staying for free, in exclusiveness away from others. I lay on my chosen bunk because it was less antsy and dozed a bit, towel, sarong underneath.

I mentioned to the others that this bed had a cold iron rail along the sides exactly as my childhood bed had. I used to heat them up with my hand so that the bed would go faster. The hand gripped on, going cold, heating up the metal rail, giving more fuel. Hands could be changed to help with the stoking, like shovelling coal, it helped to go faster. If I wanted to, I could do this all again with ease and re-live the experience of helping fire up the iron railed bed for more speed. I wonder where I was going in such a hurry!

Later we ate, again for free, chatted a bit and decided to go for a stroll before looking for tigers that evening, this excitement cut through any tiredness, Kat decided to join us too. After supper, preparations were made, torch and backpack at the ready, rested amid the post sunset, mountainous, tree filled park. We were picked up by the barefooted friendly ranger and set off into the black of night. One strong beam torch the ranger had, a dimmer torch Martin carried that lit the way and showed everything near where we were. I wasn't sure about this very much, there was no hunt, there was certainly no gun, no man eating stories either, prompted by our questioning the ranger.

Setting along the road with torches blazing, chatting merrily, adrenaline flowing, it was most exciting. Soon, as we were further from home, just the strong beam directed by the ranger's hand shone from side to side as we quietly and freely walked the road, eyes closely following the beam, looking for the infallible stripes. The walk was two hours. Martin was allowed to use the ranger's torch too, his other one scared things, said the ranger. Sandals in the cool of night, ready, loaded with cream, Jungle Juice midge repellent, we didn't get bitten by anything but the thirst to see a wild creature, taking it by surprise in the night. We thought we saw loads of things, the ranger said 'there, a tiger', we froze and peered hard at the beam, just more cracking branches, no tiger visible to me. This happened a few times. Martin saw part of one once, an antelope too was caught unexpectedly, the eyes I saw as bright flashes, a leopard for an instant, that was a definite, also a definite miss for me unfortunately. Returned back late to bed with expectant feelings for the next day's adventure.

With the ranger in the lead, we took a short stroll into the bush along Land Rover trails, off the tarmac road. It was really very hot, we had taken some water fortunately; following the barefooted ranger, we strolled through the trees and admired the country. Ants crossed the paths on many occasions, bravely marauding the trail, carrying those bits and pieces that ants do. My long hair helped with the heat, as it does with the cold, the shade was nice when we passed through some, although vegetation was not lush. The main things to see were not the spectacular safari views that I expected from this National Park, but instead more sedate vistas and on a smaller scale. I carried my camera, and as a large tree squirrel bumbled around in the branches above us, giving us the eye, I managed to capture it before it ran off. It was quite a treat. We pressed on for a few hours in the blazing heat, occasionally resting briefly for a sip of water before continuing. We had to be careful, of course, of how much we had left, fearing probable death if there was no water for too long.

We continued on relentlessly into the terrific heat of the middle of the day, were we mad dogs? No, we were lost and our only way of returning was to follow this unstoppable ranger who didn't think this was anything but pleasant. Hoping that we'd get home before collapsing, we continued on in a long circle, sometimes not caring too much about the details, feeling spaced by the heat. I regretted deciding that we'd do the slightly longer way, just a mile or few more, I was not so hot then. Just how did the ranger expect any baksheesh, no one in their right mind was going to give someone money for half killing them. Then I guess he didn't expect it. For the ranger, being close to nature and having the chance to talk with us about it, albeit in slightly limited English, must have been a good life but not a rich one.

Chapter 19

On our return we were really, totally in need of sleep, water and food and crashed out through the remaining heat of the day like sane people should. We had become exhausted and were glad of the ugly shaded building to nurse our wounds, though I doubt if the damage done righted itself for at least a week. An easy evening, eating with the other westerners, one of them coughed awfully, too many beedie said an Indian chap, he still smoked though. Other, happier people were there too, but no one else joined us in our antsy concrete block of bunks. Martin gave it some guitar, Kat and I played backgammon on my little magnetic set which was of previously unenvisaged use and we didn't feel any need to get high. In the evening, we went for a little tiger seeking walk around on the roads, not wanting to go out too far, they had been seen near to where our outlying building was only a few days ago. It was cool and exciting being out under the stars again, surrounded by the freshness of the uncrowded sanctuary.

The three of us strolled again next morning in the park, setting off on the familiar, we then took a road that was new to us, rucksack shared between us, water, we ambled and talked. We passed some habitation on our route and waved but continued, villages having huts with simple mud walls and tinderbox roofs.

As we strolled I lagged a bit, letting Martin and Kat do the talking ahead. I was approached by a Sadhu, he was an oldish bloke who followed me a little down the road, then beckoned me into the woods with a smile and shining eyes. I guessed that was a common place for Sadhus to exist in. I envisaged finding a huge established community of Sadhus living in the trees and even joining up with them, but I continued on my way and resolved as we parted to tell the others. They are holy respected men in India who have left materialism behind and embraced a spiritual life. Kat told us of one with an incredible penis, for a bottle of whisky he would bring on an erection then bend himself between his legs clamping a wooden pole so it stuck out horizontally to either side of him. On each end of the pole sat a person, lifting their feet up off the ground. The grinning Sadhu (I assume he'd grin because they seem to be like that) had performed his trick.

I started to wish slightly more that I'd gone off into the Sadhu civilisation I had imagined. I pondered and wondered much as we pressed on about my fulfilment of my spiritual enlightenment aspirations. I had been a regular fantasy role playing games player when younger, and one Middle Earth adventure had stopped, never to be continued. The whole party had diverged from the path leading through Mirkwood after one of the members had been swept off by an enormous spider. I could see that I had that same choice, this time of leaving the path of civilisation and going to the Sadhu woods of mystery.

Our walk continued at a restful pace, Kat not being terribly speedy despite having hiking boots, I was in sandals. We headed towards a cafe in a village, arriving hungry for lunch. The cafe unashamedly offered westernised things and there were westerners here too, we got chai and heartily ate our prepared food, regretting the expense of even our pricey chai. Kat was far less troubled by the money thing than us, I think her age and maturity helped, she had been out here for a few weeks longer than us too, which probably mellowed her towards greater acceptance.

An elephant soon turned up, wading in the marshy lake, a large chain and master, its freedom taken away. Westerners flocked towards it, taking photos and admiring the beast which was being encouraged to do something more spectacular than just stand there while being photographed. The trunk came in use for a cooling douse, I got the impression this was a regular thing that the elephant went through and stayed near the cafe. There was a great deal of temptation to go to touch the elephant and be closer to it, but this was a broken tourist elephant, there was nothing for me to gain from the whole show, the owner gained from collecting money from each person taking a photo. Kat decided to go out there and take a photo too, but Martin and I, having strong morals, gave it all a big miss and stayed in the shade sipping chai, stimulated to discussion regarding this awful situation in the first tourist bit of what had been a lovely park. With entertainment at a low, our mood spoiled, we looked around the village a bit then went away from it all into the quiet, overlooking the lake, got away from mosquitoes and relaxed, me lying back on the ground, eyes closed, trees above, bliss.

Later we returned back, along the road, having missed the heat of the day. We talked as we made our way. Kat had quite a bit to say, we'd meet up in an Indian restaurant in London town, to celebrate, this still is a nice idea, not done. On walking past a building, we heard the noise of kids being let out from school, hordes of them running shouting making a din, following us along the road. A friendly lot, excited by these unusual westerners, so far off the usual path, I suppose. A great crowd gathered behind us, a hundred faces of joy. I raced ahead and took a photo looking back, Martin later did the same, it was enjoyed uncaptured by Kat. They followed us, diminishing in size, we just kept going as the numbers dropped, soon our following petered out, they had all gone home. With that uplifting experience behind us, we continued gently home, back to our zone, it was only a few miles or so. We still had further plans that day, refreshing in a shower, and food got us into a good mood for the overnight trek into the outback ways of the park.

Late that afternoon we made a start, walked for many miles, barefooted ranger taking the stones, branches and twigs on the path in his stride. We stopped and looked at tracks, just for the hope of recognising them, no following intent, jackals to one side. There were grassy bits, paths and tracks, through bushiness and plains, the machete wasn't needed. Staying close behind our leader was something we heeded, found a good place to stop near the waterfront. We lay out our sheets, shared with the ranger our brought treats, and had quite simply an amazing sleep. With the river flowing by, the peace and the quiet, we were seriously out in the bush, at the mercy of tigers, who didn't seem to come to this sort of place, though ants and other creatures did. The best night sleep ever for me, and there were few mosquitoes too.

Awaking early we rolled up our sacks, ranger, Kat, Martin, and me side by side, we had decided not to push the distance today, Kat was tired. A quick snack then back onto the track for another many miles, sunny all the while. Following each other now, really in the zone, our very being was becoming accustomed and sharpened to the safari park ways. I felt I belonged but there was only this quick stay. We returned, a bit burnt, Kat admitted she'd been pushed (lightweight that she was), turning in a bit bushed. I was thinking that I'd rather like to go to another park sometime to experience again something this divine, for we were leaving that afternoon. Waving goodbye, Martin giving a donation, me doing so as well and Kat too, just what we felt prepared to pay, I suppose, for our lovely stay. Then, adieu and farewell, onto the bus and bustle and noise, feeling refreshed and more like a boy.

Chapter 20

Our friend Kat left us to go on her routed way, she had plans to stay a lot longer in this part of the world. We went on our way westwards soon finding ourselves in a small town waiting for a connecting bus. Martin and I found ourselves at a music event, so we decided to spend a few hours there and enjoy it. We sat down and took in the different acts that came on the stage, dancers and musicians, buying snacks and drinks as required. I needed something more and soon managed to score, also making a couple of new friends, hanging out with them. The sitar with tabla songs seemed to be about twenty minutes long, unhurried, with such a lovely gentle vibe, and brilliant musicianship, enjoyed in this peaceful atmosphere.

At one point after dark Martin and I walked round to the back of the stage and saw hundreds of children who were very excited at seeing two white people. Everyone was looking at us, a sea of little faces, Martin started waving and acting up for their entertainment, each gesture creating a wave of response in the crowd, smiles and waves and laughter. They were there for a children's show which was to the side of us but Martin took the limelight for a short time, working the crowd, upstaging the entertainer with his height and blonde curly hair and big smiles.

The mountains beckoned us, we travelled on, stopping on the way for one night in a small town, west of the ranges. There, Martin had a shirt tailor-made for himself, for around two pounds. We walked about a little bit, feeling that this was really stepping back out into the melee of everyday civilisation. Our wits were continually on test again as the competitiveness of just being alive among many many other people started to increase. Martin had himself measured up and was due to collect the shirt later that day. We'd checked out the bus times and knew what we were doing so enjoyed our spare time walking in the town, seeing all the time, new sights, smells and people as this different culture started to reveal more of itself to ourselves and us in turn to it. I was anti the shirt idea as I'd enough clothes to be getting on with. I hardly needed any more to carry, having already jeans, a wrap around sheet, lungi or two, medical kit, including fresh needles, swab pads, anti diarrhoea stuff, enough to save my life pending a major accident occurring to me basically.

I had been accustoming myself with beedies and was becoming interested that there were so many types to choose from in many of the stalls. They cost only a few pence in English terms, so I usually had a beedie pack with me, tucked in a pocket, and often emitted a burning bay leaf smell. I was smoking five or so a day at present, never having been a heavy smoker.

We made it along a hugely windy road in a rickety bus that was revving very high in the lowest of gears whilst ascending the mountain. To see what we were approaching from afar was a sight, the towering rocks before us through the window, flat plains abounded elsewhere, the rising being fairly steep, slightly mythical. The bus driver slammed through the gears, dodged ox-carts, beeped at anyone or anything that looked like it may have been in the way of the oncoming bus. The road was two lanes wide, tarmacked, easily wide enough for the occasional passing car, pedestrians taking the outside edge of the road.

The lorries were bright and yellow coloured, often with wording of a god or company brightly painted, the crews were most careful about them, loaded as they were to the limit, with ropes, tarpaulin and a people-full cab. The engineering must be of a high standard to make these lorries worth running, probably they keep going for years on end before a new one is decided upon, or perhaps there is not such a thing as a new lorry, I certainly did not see any. With the low wage situation being as it was, the lorries must have been worth considerably more than the drivers and crew. With this in mind, the lorries must have to have been continually repaired and maintained rather than buying a new model, labour being most cheap. They were around a third of an articulated lorry length, a cab at the front and load at the back, they seemed wider than articulated lorries, having two tyres at the front and four at the rear. There was a certain amount of appeal about riding inside a lorry cab to me, asking for a lift was unsuccessful, Martin tried.

Our bus continued to wind its way into the mountains, the progress slowed as gears were dropped and engine revs heightened still more. The driver being totally unaware of the danger that we felt at his attempts to continue on at the maximum speed the engine could give out, whatever the drop to our side and whatever the tightness of corner. When it was flat we went fast, when it was uphill we went slow. Never mind that the view out of one side is of extraordinarily steep-sided mountainside down to the next hairpin bend, and that it's certain death, no fences or barriers. After an hour or so, the fear had turned into fascination and by the summit, I was an expert and certainly enjoying the experience. So, having attained the summit without using our own legs once, the bus carried on, leaving us in welcome silence, a chilly air, Kodaikanal. The temperature had been dropping on ascent, the change was needed for it had been as hot as it gets in February. I walked around in my lungi, I did not have anything warm to put on my top, having decided anyway that I had just enough clothes.

Chapter 21

We went to a youth hostel which seemed cheap, it wasn't bad and there were nice people, westerners staying in some of the other bunks. One or two people had just arrived and other bunks had rucksacks on top of them, so we knew they would be back later on, we quickly decided that we couldn't be bothered even to look into going anywhere else, here was very nice really. The view was immense, just a short walk out of the front door of this wooden, roughly tiled roofed building and straight ahead, standing among the flowers, the plains down below. The gradually sloping hillside touching them in a spectacular view which was total vision.

We assigned ourselves a bunk each, putting our stuff on them as there was nothing else to do with it. When we considered that nobody else's had been knowingly stolen and that there were not lockers anyway, we quickly had to become used to the idea of leaving all our worldly possessions in a backpack on a bed in a room with loads of people coming in and out of it. So we did this but took our passports and money. I had two hundred pounds in fifties, for the exchange rate on a fifty was higher than smaller denominations, and the return bit of the aeroplane ticket. I had a bodybelt which was uncomfortable in the heat, this went underneath my shirt, next to my skin, after prolonged usage my passport shaped itself to my belly.

The questions emerged that so often get asked in these slightly uneasy situations, with people who want to get to know you and whom you want to get to know. Asking such mundane questions pretty much guarantees that you two are not going to get on in the first place. "Where are you from?" - "I'm from London" usually the fact that London is in England goes unexplained, many people we met had been there. They said they knew a bit in the north of it or that they had been to Hammersmith or that they even knew Chiswick, where I lived. The information was also asked by us, but when you are sitting on top of a beautiful mountain in India talking to someone with a German accent, often you don't care from which part of Germany they are from, it's hardly going to be the East as the wall was still up then. The route travelled would often be discussed, where are you going and where have you been, or how long have you been travelling were common ones. Some folk had been on the road for a year or even several years, the long-time travellers tended to be more laid back about travelling than average citizens like ourselves.

I was still excited about items that I had packed and forgotten about in pockets of my rucksack, opening the medical kit gave me a thrill. I suppose that trivialities such as these were of little consequence to a seasoned traveller, who would probably think in terms of peoples and continents rather than things in their rucksack. There were a few people, not that we had met many yet, who were currently in their third year or so of bumming it around the world.

India was one of those places within which there was little or no hope of getting any paid work, but here was always the possibility for voluntary work, as there is anywhere you choose to go in the world. People we met had travelled to America, Australia, Thailand, China, it seemed that the round the world ticket choice was a popular one, taking you to six select capital cities, always going one direction round the globe. I wondered how the passport visas were organised and what a trial it would be to get everything done before you left the country, going along, from one country to the next.

A chap John was there, he was a down to earth bloke who had managed, very casually, to take a sizeable lump of hashish with him from Nepal to the south of India. He'd just been carrying it around and had passed through customs, he gave the impression that he had pretty much just remembered about this lump. I'd not seen hash since England, it all seemed to be grass here in India. I had a bit with me from Kovalam, this we stuffed into John's chilum which Martin was keen to try, as was I, it being a more traditional way to inhale the smoke. This had quite a drastic effect on our senses, being out of it after a hit or two each, the chilum having to be kept continually alight with a gas lighter, it not being packed right. The sweet dope, along with grass and a little tobacco thrown in was an unusual and successful mix, Martin and I enjoying being stoned, while the other chap was more cool about it.

Our thinking was that it was crazy and mad and definitely fun to become headless on the effect of a chilum, John seemed to have a calmer, more blissed-out reaction and attitude to taking it, I thought him rather cool actually. He told us about a deep ravine mountain pass that takes you into Nepal from India, a long ascent into the mountains, sheer on each side, he thought first that we had been there, we became quickly very relaxed, enjoying the late evening feeling. Martin turned into bed and I sat outside to view the extraordinary clear sky which revealed so many stars. The whole sky at once could be seen from here, overawing me with the enormity of the scene that the stars laid out, with the horizon below me.

Chapter 22

We decided to eat out the next evening, and four of us with chilum John walked in the night, I having donned sensibly warm jeans for the occasion. We looked into a few places along the road, a little way from the youth hostel, and decided upon one of them, just a normal unexciting cafe place with people in it. That said, there were two unusual people near to us, a spiritual couple, they talked between themselves. They each had a look to them, seemed to me to be similar to gypsies dressed as goths in England, scarves, silver jewellery, dark tops and trousers, definitely westerners. They were of interest to me as they dressed as you do in the west and took little notice about how everyone else did. They took my mind back to bars and places in London and, in many ways, I think they helped me feel homely. I looked at them a lot during the course of the evening. We were not deeply involved in conversation, the dope took care of that, instead it had a slightly hallucinogenic quality about it, these dark, interesting goth gypsy strangers made it that bit more memorable.

The meal was average. Martin and I budgeted as usual, John had an expensive choice, later regretting it. As we had nearly finished our meal and were drinking post-pudding chai, a chap who had been making conversation in another part of the pub came over to us, wanting to talk. He was insane, on an extraordinary high and full of himself, he spoke fast and enthusiastically. I chatted with him seriously whilst John tried to take the piss. He came nearer and didn't sit down but talked with us for around a quarter of an hour. His name was Superfast and he worked as a guide, we could go with him on some mountain trails, I guess for an afternoon or even a couple of days if we wished. Pam, an English woman with us, asked the inevitable question, would you really want to go walking with him, her point being that she did not feel safe with a guy pumped full of drugs and every bit showing it.

He said in his fast, cool tone that he told his mother he couldn't go home to her because he was catching flights, was it airplanes he was referring to or possibly cocaine which could have made him Superfast. Whatever his mum wanted him to do, he had to stay away, he was convinced that this was his mission. I slightly embarrassed everyone else by being so friendly with him, talking with that guy in the busy cafe. Despite the fact that I may have tarnished my reputation, I did not give a shit as I had enjoyed breaking down social barriers by speaking with him. I said I'd like to go with him on a walk somewhere, and knowing his name I could contact him.

None of the others were really into it though and the idea fell flat on its face, as regrettably I did not have the confidence to go with Superfast by myself. I imagined he would take loads of drugs to sustain him for the journey, I guessed that him in the mornings was probably an unpleasant experience. The amount of drugs that must have been in his bloodstream that evening, that had turned him into a frenzied socialising monster, must have meant that he had difficulties and I envisaged myself being able, at last, to try all sorts of drugs, previously untried by myself. This idea seemed exciting to me at the time, a breakthrough of barriers, a lawless zone, with a law-unabiding person giving me absolute drug-trying freedom. I just didn't quite fancy it however and so it never came off.

Chapter 23

We thought about how to fill the next day, the guidebook didn't help much with little things, but we knew where to go. The town had holiday accommodation, advertised richly, a market area and spread out parts. We passed a radio mast through hundreds of Eucalyptus trees, the smell was intense and must have cleaned me out and detoxified. I bought some oil which kept its smell for months, even with the lid closed, this effect was enough. There was plenty for sale, but really I didn't know what to do with it, just that I liked the smell. We also vaguely tried to find the old woman we heard about down at the market who sold magic mushrooms, dried, because they were out of season.

There was a winding path which led round the mountain, along it we walked, through forest, the area was slightly English, it having been developed in Raj times. The fascination of the English at recreating their home environment which they had left was of interest to me, why not just stay at home, saving the Indians a lot of bother? Other places which were in the guidebook had had this done to them in major ways, with English villages and snooker halls existing. The mishmash culture of India certainly had room for such eccentric sections, I suppose that the familiarity was comforting to someone like myself thousands of miles away from home. The path continued on, westerners walking arm in arm, strolling restfully down the thin path of stones for a long view down the mountain.

One morning I made it up early and sat outside, intensely regarding the scene in front, it was a room of slumber inside. A lady was there from France, about in her forties. I studied the mountains in such a way that I looked at one spot for a bit then moved onto the next. The effect was that I can remember now the gradual change in formation from grass to rock as the hillside lowered to the planes. I had not brought my camera along as there were plenty of days to capture this regular spectacle. We chatted a bit, the two of us outside, she was a city person, I tried out some French. We were joined by Pam whom I proudly told that I'd been up for an hour already, I was trying to make her jealous that she had got up so late and missed the opening of the sun. Pam had been watching for a while from inside through the window but realised that it was much better out here for seeing things. It was an experience to be revelled in, I rarely see sunrise, it is really worth doing, and at a panoramic spot the gradual warming of the clouds on the planes and in the valleys is easily seen.

I did not feel the need to go back to sleep but seriously considered having a hit of grass. Martin thought I was silly, I thought I was outrageous, and did it anyway, meeting the rest of the day with a dreamy aloofness, which meant that Martin had to make decisions about things we were to do together. Breakfast, not talking much, we did our own thing in the day, for the first time I was aware of Martin's need for independence and my expectation that we'd want to do everything together. I cared a lot about Martin, I was less responsible, we both gained from our friendship. We had been together in school and out, at each other's houses, playing games, cycling together, parties and fun for a number of years.

Chapter 24

While reading, I got given a book that was modern, listing some of India's problems, there were two women walking on the cover carrying fruit on their heads. I thanked the traveller for donating to me something of hers and apologised that I couldn't give her any of my books as I had not yet read them. I never did read it though, I later gave it to somebody else without opening the thing. I did feel the generosity was great, that someone so far away from home, who didn't have much, would want to give me something and think nothing of it. She was a laid back, typically cool traveller type who was wise in making so little of a scene that I felt to be important.

I had purchased a bamboo recorder, called a flute, but not really a flute, from a place we stopped off at on our way. There were loads in a basket, I had pulled a few out and blew them, taking the one with the sound I most liked. I decided to venture again down the path and then walked off of it, I was in one of my meditative moods, on pause whilst the world rushed on by. I did not actually meditate with eyes closed and chant, but instead sat on a rock, looking through the trees to a path which was uncrowded. I played tunes which came into my head, having done this lots at the ashram, I played easily for a hour or so.

I was however still acutely shy, and seeing a person walking along the path turn round to look in my direction made me falter, just knowing this one person was tuning into me put me off altogether. I did carry on after that but had another interruption. The trees behind me rustled and a monkey dropped to the ground, looking at me from about ten yards away. I tried to play on, but again, was nervous at the monkey audience member being there, sorry monkey. I knew them already to be like humans in very many ways, being alone with this one upset my playing totally though and I had to go back soon after trying again to start up. Imagine if I'd been able to continue and hypnotise the monkey with my charming music! Not likely, you may say, but I felt that that was just a breath away. I paced back, feeling again calm and fortified, this was a trick I was learning to do well, the tranquillity there in the forest, augmented by the sounds of my flute, real peace, a beautiful place in the mountain air, not easy to go and find by sitting down in the local park.

Chapter 25

An Australian guy, John, and his girl, a Dead Head (a travelling fan of the Living Dead band), lived in the more select outer cottages, renting their own abode. The attractive, long brown haired, Californian girl spoke really enthusiastically about things, 'I reckon' was her phrase. Probably her energy lifted the deep, slow John who was a bong head, smoking grass grown near to him when in Australia. Martin and he shared a guitar playing interest, though John could make up his own songs, something that I had not yet seen from Martin. We hung around with them at their place one evening smoking pot and chatting, playing guitars, me on my flute recorder. A French-ish lady called Katia who had been on the road for around two years hung out too, with five or so in our group on the floor, late in the relaxing evening, we were unknowingly tape recorded by her. The music brought us together, we who knew each other barely, having travelled thousands of miles to be there, it felt like a family with loving music to soothe.

That smoky evening I remember seeing Martin for the first time as a sad fellow behind the happy guitar playing, I had at last seen through the facade. I wrote about the deep insight in my diary but it's still in India and the little attempt I made to retrieve it has long failed. The thing about Martin, my close friend and companion, was that he was always entertaining and that evening I believe I worked out why. He had to cheer people and lift the atmosphere around himself because he needed it to survive, himself being sad inside.

The party ended. I had made a rather cool friend, John the bong man. We tried out a few hits on the water bong of his, he didn't seem to smoke tobacco atall. The couple had been travelling for a number of months together and it was nice to share their love with them. She had only one medium rucksack and wore denim jeans and a jacket continually. She'd seen a lot, I imagined, but I wondered how much of the real street life, the real low down people in India, she had seen. I certainly wished to fully experience as much of that as I could, as for me that was what India was so much about. The television documentaries of bicycles on the streets, alongside oxen and hordes of people everywhere are totally realistic. I felt as the trip went on, that people in India are an organism working with one another, whereas in the west the competitive edge makes the individuals get ahead and the organism as a whole falls behind. I really do think that some places like India and, I imagine, many other third world places provide a better quality of life, as experienced by being a part of an organism rather that an individual in one's own right. This individualistic striving here in the west only falsely succeeds if you look close enough.

We did a trek the next day, trying to reach a village that was in the Lonely Planet guide, six of us went after breakfast along the path and out into the wilderness more. Many of the party I knew very vaguely, Martin seemed to know what he was doing here and I tagged along and chatted. The view was continually magic down to our left, a forest with a mist above it was ahead and below. We stopped for a break and I went away from the rest of the group, playing my recorder, being slightly put out when someone approached me and said that it was nice music that I was making. I carried on playing, minding less now about sharing my mood with another, my playing was different, not accompanying in a crowded room but now tuneful and leading.

Onwards we pressed, my inner-self now revealed to somebody. A really rooted path was a feature of the walk, the trees lining the path had spread their roots so that a stairway existed of thick wood. The path was three or four people wide and had soil between the lightly raised roots. It was a fantastic path to walk on, not a stone in sight and to be walking in our sandals on the tender roots of these old enormous trees was an honour. We walked along the edges of cultivated gardens on the hillside, much less tree-laden but obviously cared for nonetheless. We didn't manage to reach the village, the leaders of the trek couldn't figure it out from the scanty map, I didn't get involved knowing full well that Martin was the better direction finder. So returning home, we make the most of the walk, a change from this place, which I felt was a bit touristic and catering very much for the visitor. We had managed to get to some of the more backstreet parts of the town and have a smoke, however.

Chapter 26

That evening we walked into town and sat in a park, after dark, having some of what was being passed around. I chatted with a law student and thought him good to try expanding his mind with a bit of blow in addition to his studies, which could only surely close his mind off to the world after all. Perhaps we felt a common bond at being unfulfilled and needing to get high to conquer the fact that we weren't learning what was necessary for us in what we'd decided to do. My decision was possibly leading me down the wrong path, I had chosen to go to Leeds university to do an Engineering course and here I was in India, loosely following the footsteps of both my grandfathers who had done engineering in India in Raj times. Hydroelectric projects and the like. I'd not planned to see any projects they had been involved in but pursued instead an interest in society, specialising in people, needing to be alone sometimes of course as well.

There was quite a bunch of us in the park. I asked and was assured that no one was going to bother to throw us out for being there at night. It made me realise that here we were, sitting on some grass, on a mountainside, smoking and chatting in the night, near to the main road and were completely free to do so and enjoy ourselves. It's no wonder that I wished to experience this freedom, having been shut away in London at school for too long, obeying those silly rules for so many years.

I got thinking about the big bang that started off the universe and how the explosion was still moving outwards. Surely all the gravity of all the suns and planets was going to attract everything slowly back together again and make another big bang. Some of the outermost pieces of the explosion would not get drawn into the next big bang, they would escape. A long, long repeated cycle of creation and destruction of countless planets, suns and lives evolved over countless years. I thought this rather profound and could visualise it all.

The next day John was going to try out a motorbike, he was thinking seriously of buying one, an old British Enfield for a cheap price. He managed to borrow it for a day and in the morning I caught up with him and we went for a ride together, no tax, insurance or helmets, along the road, avoiding busy routes. Turning off, having sped down the road, we sat for a bit under trees looking out at the vista unending and I said "how about a little smoke" which was a great idea. A spliff later of stuff which I had produced, we were chatting in a more casual way before I was allowed to ride the thing home with John on the back. I tried to swerve it to avoid potholes in the road and nearly lost it, giving myself a fright, I yelled apologetically to John who said he thought it was funny. The front suspension fluid in the forks wasn't there, and each bump made the forks go to their limit making a nasty bang which damaged the bike more and more, every jolt, poor handling. The engine was not powerful enough for serious acceleration, feeling loose, altogether a bad and dangerous buy. He declined the option to buy and in effect hired the thing instead for just a day. This trip with John was great. I really wanted him to know that I thought a lot of him and valued highly all the time I spent with him as it felt rich and special, he was so friendly and laid back that I felt positively invited whenever I turned up.

A young blond Brazilian girl had turned up at the hostel and I had been told that she fancied me, not by her though, she seemed sixteen and full of life. I had been looking at the talent here and had noticed her but imagined her as being from a destitute, deprived Brazilian background and, anyway, she seemed a handful of energy to cope with. I did chat with her a tiny bit, knowing full well that I was leading her on, as we sat on the steps of the hostel in the company of others. I didn't want anything to happen immediately, but was content in the knowledge that she fancied me and she was good looking. Someone else later mentioned to me the same fact so I was really sure that she was charmed.

Martin managed to get his Walkman fixed at a market stall, with his detective ability he found a guy who did the work for a small fee, the electronics were bust. The chap had lots of letters of thanks from westerners to whom he had proved his worthiness, after returning a day later the Walkman was repaired. If Martin had asked me to do something about it I would have confidently said that I could fix it and may have turned the machine to a worse state of repair, as I've done at home many times, not sharing the same fixing patience as my father.

Chapter 27

I had managed to obtain a sachet of grass from a local dealer, 'my man' I called him, it took a few meetings for us to arrange the exchange, I got a handful of grass in a plastic bag for 35 rupees (a quid). Afterwards I walked with my prize, with Martin and others to a secluded area and sat around in the sun, we had a picnic and my grass was refused so it didn't get started. On returning back, I just couldn't find the sachet anywhere, not in pockets or rucksack, and later that day I went back and searched in vain for my bounty. I didn't find it and returned home disheartened. It seemed so important to find the treasure but I doubt that finding it would have been quite as much joy as the expectation that had built up in my mind. Searching through the reeds, on the grassy areas, in the secluded walks that we'd played about on, just nowhere, and I didn't even enjoy my searching walk but left with heavy sinking heart at the loss.

Another day we walked into town and saw the hotels with signs written promising the luxuries and the price for them, this was Indian Tourism. It gave me a new perspective on tourism. I thought how like sheep these guests must be, with little thought for what they really wanted to do perhaps. The whole idea of package holidays repulses me, I've been on organised trips of sorts, always with an optional degree of individual freedom involved. The disparity was extreme between the safe hotel holidays up on the mountain, with all the mod cons from home, and the wandering backpack lifestyle, with home being temporary place to temporary place. This generally made me feel more exciting and interesting than these others who had gone so little out of their comfort zone for their holiday.

In front of one hotel was a painted sign reading 'Road Mishaps' recounting the number of road related fatalities, injuries and bumps people had received last year. The figures were a couple hundred deaths etc. but I did not find out about the area covered so I've no idea if they were proportionally high, they would be enormous if just for the area up on the mountains in the vicinity.

Through Martin, who knew this guy through speaking a few times with him, we went to see a German hippy bloke Billy who'd been in India since the sixties, smoking ganja and living on expiring visas. Now his visa was close to finishing again and he had plans to make it back, saving money by selling twisted wires as jewellery. He was hard of hearing so conversation was a real effort, I didn't try as hard as Martin who was quite taken with him. Billy said he'd got a present of a Walkman and was really glad that he could listen to music on it, the neighbours were probably pleased at the absence of a loud tape deck. He was thin, wrinkly, with bangles and bracelets which I did not take to much, but I did like the weathered look he had obtained, really earthy and old looking, a little beard, sparkling eyes. I knew he'd seen more and done more, living in poverty, and other types of down to earth real life things than I'll ever do, so many stories he could have told.

He didn't tell us any when we went back to his house, he listened to music, asking us what bands we liked. Although he knew of the old ones such as The Doors, he wasn't all that sure about some of the newer band names we came up with. With his hearing aid switched on, things started to roll a bit more, he could hear us, the tape deck could go on now as it was not going to make quite so much noise, and the chilum came out. A large American guy who seemed rich and arrogant, loaded the chilum, packing it tight. Once lit, it was passed round, always the same direction to keep Ganesh happy. We puffed and yes it was a powerful hit, I did not smoke hard but tasted, Billy had a go and was repulsed by the fact that tobacco had been used to load the chilum and told the American off. We finished that off anyway and I could tell Billy was displeased as he thoroughly cleaned the chilum after that load had gone. The chilum, a hollow cone of stone, had an elephant on the side of it. To clean, a thin rag was posted right through and pulled tight, the chilum was moved back and forth and revolved around whilst moving to get all the gunk and tar out. The blackened cloth also came in use for a bottom filter to put over the chilum where you suck from the thin end, stopping any falling debris from being tasted.

The chilum was not his largest, he showed us that one but did not use it, it had a snake and eagle on the side and inscription which had been made for him, personalising the artefact. The next time, the chilum was loaded purely with grass from Billy and Martin, about an eighth of an ounce. Traditional rules and regulations being observed. Billy initiated the fire with a lighter and took a lungful of smoke, making the top burn red with a glow. He held his breath for a bit, passing the chilum on to the next person, to the right, a few seconds later he gently exhaled his lungful, releasing a cloud of smelly burnt grass into the room. The American's turn next, then mine, I took the chilum, deciding that I was going to compete with Billy, taking a much larger-than-before suck on the stone chilum. I could barely hold the thing properly and could not take a lungful but did manage to hold my breath, solemnly passing the thing on to the willing Martin. Exhalation, throat okay, no bits in the mouth and whoosh, this time I was beginning to come up on the grass. Billy then the American had it again and I had another pull before the fire died out. We sat for a little while, me chatting with the American, finding out that he was a businessman in the States. Martin paid more attention to Billy. We listened to some more music then drifted out of the shack, with me unknowing of the way back, I followed Martin who knew, discussing quite how very stoned we were feeling together.

Billy was a hippy who never made it back, the guidebook warns of the bad reputation some of these drifting drug heads have on Indian society, that they are scorned by the Indians and are thought of as a nuisance. Not Billy, he was kind and gentle, making jewellery showed his self sufficiency, Martin bought some. I felt sorry that he was so far away from his German home and so hopelessly out of touch with the place that had changed so much, that he had to go back was the saddest part of his story.

We visited Katia too, she was not staying at the hostel and had a shared house, many foreigners there, a water pump in the back garden, mosquito nets hung in one of the rooms, hardcore travellers they must have been. One net was complicated and made a four poster bed-like space on the normal bunk. She had a single room, far more classy than our dorm room, we did not enter but sat outside in the back garden area. Martin read some of Katia's writings, regarding the experiences that you have everyday when in India and living the Indian lifestyle. The place was pleasant. Katia seemed very organised, doing her own washing and cleaning, something I had given little thought or attention to, letting my clothes become quite dirty before paying someone to wash them and moving out of a hotel room before it needed cleaning. Katia shared a washing tip in her writings, a bucket of water with clothes in, keeping the tap on for an hour to wash them clean, I hid my shock at this wasteful method employed.

Chapter 28

The day of leaving was time for me to bid goodbye to the friends at the hostel, bye to them who'd turned up at the bus, bye especially to John and his loud and proud Californian girlfriend. I had gone down to their place and said farewell, I'm just about to leave on the bus, John said 'Oh I was going to ask you if you wanted another bong with me before you go'. I chose not to spend more time with the guy, who was one of the coolest I had ever met, my journey rolled on. I had no desire at present to travel apart from Martin, and anyway we'd made a plan to go.

Pam had given me a t-shirt with the arms ripped off, with a red dog barking on the centre, I did not have anything to put on my top so that was good of her. I don't know what I had done with my tops, she must have felt sorry for me but I think there was a begging element involved in my not wearing anything on my top and being too disorganised to do anything about it. I wore it now on the bus.

There was Pam, and Katia, Martin and myself, it was a scorching hot day, the bus cooking inside. Martin and I put our rucksacks on the seats, then waited outside for a bit in the relative cool. The bus began to fill up and at last we climbed into the oven as the horn started telling us of impending departure. The blonde Brazilian girl said goodbye and smiled, me also at her. I asked her for some fags and she gladly gave me a packet of them. I thanked her for her generosity and left regretting slightly the non-physical aspect of our relationship. I thought that to be with a girl in India travelling anywhere you wanted meant real freedom, like some lovers walking hand in hand down a path that I'd seen one day, like John and his girlfriend, exploring together. It would have been a change from hanging around with Martin but that was all, probably. The temptation that I'd let fly was a rare thing for me to do, usually working hard to be as successful as possible with the girls.

So here I was, going towards Madurai city with two women, no thought of a sexual relationship, on a mission of finding wisdom with the aid of the ancient spiritual herb marijuana, to lead me onwards. The idea of speaking with wise men and meeting all sorts of people I pushed and pursued, my social exploits had been colourful for years, so talking to the many Indians who I came into contact with was a natural thing for me to do, being of an extroverted personality.

The ride was a few hours, the wind started to cool us, bums sticking to the seat, the journey was great, views out of the window which Martin was next to. Conversation was most limited as the bus made such a noise, our fares of five Rupees (fourteen pence) would take us all the way to Madurai, the sign on the front of the bus, so there was no need to enquire when we should get off.

The plains were hot, the temperature rising as we descended, this time using the engine purely as a brake the whole way down, slowing the careering, full bus round the hairpins edged by drops of death. I wondered how the lorries were getting on, burdened with weight on their way down, low gear, high revs, engine braking. Some were stopped on their descent, crew members around the vehicle applying water to the burdened, possibly red hot brakes that had to rest now and then, making the descent a slow and tedious but safer one. At some corners an escape safety path went off to stop careering lorries, we'd not noticed these on our way up. The escape space was not a road but a grassy verge, the lorries sometimes went onto this part slightly as the bus whizzed round the corner, overtaking in the inside space, before the lorry turned slowly back onto its path, and we'd left the slow beast of burden behind.

The plains were flat, rice farmers tended the land, a monotonous mosaic of rectangular fields of paddy rice, also some cereal crops, but noticeably a limited variety of food to choose from. I was sitting near the window now, enjoying the country. Hard working peasants walked on the road and could be seen in the fields, I took a couple of clear photos and enjoyed the view. Arriving through the increasingly busy streets, the noises got louder, horns bleeping in many places. Intense heat with little wind greeted us, stepping out of the tin can oven of a bus, leaving it empty, soon there were peanut sellers and other folk asking us if we wanted to buy. They were asking us at the wrong time, tired and pissed off at their demands, Martin asked them sarcastically if they knew where a hotel was which we could stay in. We hunted and with little difficulty found digs.

  The hotel was a grandiose one, expensive and plush and by no means unaffordable, I objected at it being too posh, then followed Martin and the others in. We placed our bags in a secure storage room and paid a few rupees for the privilege, I took my most prized body belt from the bag and off we went for some lunch and to see the sights of this bustling religious city. Popping into a nearby cheap restaurant was easy for us now. Rice was expected, fried wheat pancakes sometimes came too, however the food was not hot, not anywhere was it spicy hot here. Spicy sauces and yoghurt accompanied the usually vegetarian meals. Lassi was the nicest thing to drink, cool creamy, melted ice cream in milk, it came in beakers and I drank it, even though it must have been diluted with water from the local source. This was strongly and commonly advised to be avoided at all times and instead to carry around a stupid plastic bottle of pure water. We drank lassi quite happily as it was mostly not water and tasted really nice as well as cooling us down.

  Wandering leisurely through the streets was enjoyable, stopping now and then for a new packet of beedies or matches, a cup of chai, if there is a destination in mind the trip is more channelled. Katia was a pro, journalist that she was, she looked out for unusual and interesting bits on her journey. Some things that she picked up on were of the more everyday and mundane that soon become accepted by westerners in India, through lack of any other choice. I never understood or asked what magazine she wrote for, to me, she seemed to be using that as an excuse to travel anywhere, taking photos and writing. At least she had a focus for the information she was gathering, she managed to process things as she went, it seemed.

Chapter 29

Back to the hotel, and Martin, good on him, had the energy to sort out the rooms with the hoteliers, having stored our stuff with them earlier helped, at last, with our keys, three separate rooms, Martin and I together. We went to Pam's and ate crisps like monsters, scoffing our faces, having a snack attack lunch. Pam didn't smoke but Katia did, it was fun before turning in. After seeing again, city poverty and human despair I think we were driven to pig out with the crisps as a defence, smoking was that too, a dulling of the pain felt at our surroundings.

The following day we walked out again, bravely into the incredibly hot day, this was not summer but the heat was enough to make tiredness set in after an hour in the shine. I was not a mad dog though an Englishman, so I tried to keep to the shade mostly and not go out in the midday sun. Martin and I stuck together, we saw some plastic imitation decoration things that took our fancy, deciding to look elsewhere and come back to this stall near to the hotel, we walked around, eating, enjoying. Later that week we bought five pens each from the stall, greedily. I purchased a little lined hardback book and began to write in the occasional thing with India ink and Indian fountain pen, "Aaron's thoughts in India". Martin too got a book another day and wrote too.

We went on a bus to places, now having mastered the throng and sussed out the city of Maduri from our guidebooks more. For us to walk the streets then to squeeze onto an already full bus which careered off through the heavy traffic was okay now. The bus horns blared as the traffic beeped, the manoeuvring tactics, roundabouts worked with a steady stream as did junctions. The roads were crowded, buses, taxis, rickshaws, bicycles, pulled rickshaws of the non-motorised kind, not forgetting the cars of the rich bods. It was chug and grind in the city but we felt alive, siesta was out for today, photos were in, Katia having a camera and the skill and determination to use the thing. She encouraged me to take mine out with me, she took so many pictures, having it always around her neck. The city sight rolling by out the window, bright colours of godly things made of man-made things, flowers, tinselly things, stalls that sold loads of them.

Rickshaws tended to be decorated in stickers with bright material strands hung across the windows, I didn't ride in a really well done one and the back was often less plush and uncomfortable inside. On view for the driver, he could look upon a range of gods as he drove and passengers could see a bit out of his window, the jungle of traffic surrounding. More could be seen easily if we looked out of the side at the road running past and the street life at the low level from our seat. A luxury rickshaw existed providing better seating arrangements but by and large they were all of the same design, making a mechanic's life an easy one.

Chapter 30

We decided to go to the major sized temple which the bus had
passed on the way here, not far away. The guidebook told of a guided
tour of brilliant lights and mystic moons, we opted just to wander at our
own free will, no cost, indulging in the taking of photographs. I kept my
shoes on for the outer courtyard area which was reached by passing
through an arch in the outer boundary wall. Four gated towers guarded
the temple, they were huge, one of them such a monster of carved
stonework that a modern day estimate for labour costs in the west is
incalculable. The walls had red and white paint along the tops of the
outside brightening the thing up a bit, this made me feel more like
visiting. There were flat stones to walk on around the outer square,
people inside sit and some chat. I was offered by one guy to go into the
mountains and play drums with him, he wanted to teach me how to
play. If I'd said yes then the decision would have been okay and the trip
would have meant that Martin and I may have met up again later on.
But I didn't, even though I fancied the idea and assumed the chap to be
trustworthy regards his promise, mainly because I met him in the
temple.

Indians respect religion and temples, that they are an integral
part of things showed how much the people respect their faith. It was a
Hindu temple, carvings typically organically complex, consisting of
numerous figures, monsters, mythological beasts and gods all of the
Hindu dynasty, all hand carved in stone. The effect was a huge 3-D
mosaic of intertwining heads and bodies, individual faces could be seen
although only at the lower end, as you looked higher, the faces faded

and became organic, part of the general effect whilst not being individually distinguishable. On the summit of the tower were winged beasts, the crescent shape of them becoming stunning at sunset as their dark silhouette fell against the sky. I went many times to the temple, passing through sometimes into the inner parts, seeing rituals with my friends Katia and Martin.

It is strange seeing people walk round a glass case with a model of the three dimensional spacing of the planets in the solar system and them all walking around the same way, being with the way of the world and blessing themselves as they completed the circuit. It was as if by looking at the model and being near to it, a blessing was put onto the worshipping members of the public that bothered to inspect it. The gods were represented in the planets and so most folk could relate to it.

I was given a fingertip smudge of redness by a priest, between my eyes and felt part of the faith and accepted into the atmosphere presiding. I wore it for the rest of the day, proud that I had been blessed and proud that I was a humble westerner who got a blessing. Many of the Indians around had not made the effort to go to the temple and get a red fingerprint on them but instead had homemade affairs that lacked the significance. The reason for this was that they were, all of them, working their socks off in the jobs they had and did not have the time or energy to go daily. It seemed to me that the Hindu religion works on an 'anytime is okay to worship' principle, so you just turn up to the temple, say your prayers, sing a chant from a book or whatever then go away when you felt like it. A nicer aspect that, than Christianity.

A day when I looked around with Katia we saw into more parts of the inner temple. Peace we found here quite easily and felt fine about walking around wherever we wished, there not being much official pomp and circumstance to get in our way. I sat down after long wandering, within earshot of an old man who had a book opened on his lap, chanting prayers written there. I did not feel moved to photograph, but just to watch intensely and listen to him. The effect was magical, such ancientness, an old wrinkled, thin, weather beaten, gnarled guy singing beautifully and surely. Katia came by asking me about going onwards, taking photos, she was far more in the photo mood than I that day, clicking regularly. I said I'd like to stay, sit, listen and do nothing, and she left me by myself whilst I continued to be immersed in this melody of old. It was slow, sure, reassuringly tedious, but with a few points of interest to it, a song that comforted me. I talked about it afterwards with Katia saying that I had been moved, but she didn't get off on it the same way I did, I dropped the matter quickly.

One day some music played on reedy pipes drifted out, a procession of priests, dressed in their red garb. A procession of brass bits, a gong being gonged, shiny metals, chains holding the incense, smoking the place as they walked fast along the corridors, past us, waiting on the side. I thought sometimes that some things were not right to take photos of and this was an occasion, as it was deep inside the temple and I thought that they might mind. Probably it didn't matter at all to them what went on as long as they could walk where they were going and do what they were doing. Along the corridor, pipes monotonously blaring, gong crashing, anti-melodic, un-rhythmic, chaotic and beautiful to take in, this had been done for centuries and who knows for how many centuries more would it be done. The ritual was never the same twice, it was always different, so it was always changing, unlike a recording, they go through different movements, different actions, different notes played, each procession. The sound was free and wild like this, they swept with presence past us, noise a maximum when they were near, and on, along on down, through the place, spreading their chaotic noise whenever they went.

Another time as the evening became dark I walked inside the temple, round the whole outer perimeter and saw an elephant, a temple elephant. It was standing calmly, people going back and forth, keepers nearby, a spiritual creature in a spiritual place. Though I did not feel it was right to keep an elephant in service in this way I was entranced by the magic of the animal and drew nearer. I stood a metre away, looking into its left eye, we stared at each other for a long look. I did not want to touch it as it felt wrong and invasive, instead I stood calmly and took in the experience of being so near this incredible animal. The calmness and sureness it exuded had a powerful effect on me. I felt it had let me take a deep look into its soul, where there was stillness. This elephant seemed to bring peace to the temple, it seemed to be the most important thing there and the most powerful too, both in mind and body. I walked on, deeply touched by my experience of this communion with that patient, powerful elephant.

Chapter 31

The museum of the history of Gandhi lay on the outskirts of town. I knew that he'd done a great deal of good, in a similar way to Jesus I supposed, so off I went. The bus dropped me off for a few pence, kitted out for the day, I strolled into the museum and had a look. There was art here, old and modern, some modern stuff had been done with just a few strokes or a running effect of the paint upon the canvas caused by water dilution, they were inspired works. I took the liberty of taking a few photos as I thought them so good, prints and postcards being unavailable.

The exhibition had little Ganesh statuettes and other gods in glass cases, all bunched together with labels on some of them giving the date of origin. These meant little more to me than lumps of metal that were idol worshipped, however the patterning on them was complicated and ornate, great skill and time had gone into them. Unfortunately some had decayed and did not make for exciting exhibits, I recorded with my camera one of the larger metal sculptures. A shiny, black, curvy, large breasted woman with snakes all around her, doing a dance, done in the Hindu way. The modern statues of today seemed much the same as yesterday, no striking difference, the designs did not seem to have evolved, they did look good however.

The Gandhi bit lay further through, a series of panels leading round a hall, they stood like sentries and could be easily read. The entire history from birth to death with a vast record of achievements was there, what a guy. He lead the way to huge political upheaval and change, after he had inspired the people to fight the common enemy with peace. The British didn't have a hope with so many people simply getting in the way of the authorities, even being killed as they sat obstructing. The regime was broken, the Brits went away and quickly, amid the chaos, the spaces of power were filled, led by Gandhi. He was a politician through and through, so popular with the people as he dressed like them and lived among them, relating to them. After this he had tried hard to change things in a political manner, visiting London, chatting, in his white loincloth, sandals and glasses. He did look odd in a picture with the White House officials. I wondered how much of a factor his dress sense was in affecting westerners' acceptance of his political arguments and aspirations.

The whole thing really fascinated me. Notably the passive and constructive resistance to the violent oppression, proving that non-violence wins, there being less blood spilled too. Having become dazed, I'd taken a water flask and sandwich break so the exhibition was done in two bits, taking over two hours to read about this great guy. Did you know he fasted himself to death, protesting the segregation of the land area into Pakistan and India, rather than one nation? The area was divided by religion, Muslim Pakistan and Hindu India, the division exists today, with a mix in each country. Whilst I was there, a person or two came and went, leaving me engrossed with Gandhi who decided not to have sex when he was older, and claimed that he could resist even the greatest of temptation.

Chapter 32

I walked outside in the sun and looked at the sky, blue, a really white cloud was making its way across the sky and was isolated, alone, a miniature cloud that could in its entirety be captured with a single photograph, it had character. I was in no rush to return to the big city. I walked, it was not too hot, filling the water bottle from a tap at the museum, walking was, something Gandhi did a great deal of.

Across the river was a huge bridge, the road was heavily used, there was a safe pavement to walk upon amid the rumble with a view to my side, of the river beneath. The walls of the bridge were red and white stripes, they ran for ages along the top of the wall in the straight line of the bridge, the thin pavement was not commonly used. Unusually, I did not pass or see anyone all the way along the bridge as I walked. The reason for this was that over to the side was another bridge, this had lots of tiny arches all the way along, it was very low and close to the water. Rickshaws, bicycles and people swarmed on it, crossing in every direction, from high up here the busy congestion looked beautiful, the shiny glistening of metal catching the sun.

The river was a delta here, making it wide, shallow and slow to cross, on a raised island bit was a ruined temple, this area was being used by a large number of people, mainly brightly coloured women, in their saris. This was a washing place, today a neighbourhood of people had turned out and were busily bashing their clothes upon the rocks with vigour to get them clean. No visible bubbles flowed away from the river, denoting washing powders having been used. I imagine the whole crowd were there, taking out their aggression onto the rocks, getting the clothes clean, wearing the rocks smooth over decades of usage and getting new ones in now and then. The bright spectacle was not unlike a shoal of fish amid the water, it was as if the town had spilled out into the river on the outskirts and was resisting being swept downstream by the bashing of the clothes.

Onwards to the other side. The camera came out again, having captured the low busy bridge, I turned my attention to wandering. Looking out for snaps to take, I walked along the road near to the river for a while, trying to locate a restaurant for a rest, some water and food, but instead I found the Munster's house or one that looked just like it. This mansion was an ancient spooky style, pointed arched windows, green and dark, utterly unlike any other I'd seen in India, such an oddity, I just had to capture it.

On the other side of the road some work had been done slapping shit onto the wall to dry, perhaps a hundred pancakes had been made and slapped, leaving a handprint in each one, none had fallen off. I took a photo of that as well, as the camera was out, it was inconvenient to constantly get in and out the bag. The shit was just left there with no one looking after it, when dry it could be burnt, the most likely event, or it could be transported elsewhere, being light, and become fertiliser material. The way the shit blended in with the wall I liked, it did not seem out of place, surely it would have in my street, there would have been outcry to have the stuff removed, but as it was for the common good it stayed. I had walked a long way up this road in search of a watering hole and turned back, mission unsuccessful, to continue along the path towards the city, the bus and my friends there.

Chapter 33

Madurai is a large city, holding more than can be visited in the week or so I was there. Katia and I went exploring in quite some detail and discovered for ourselves a fair bit. One day we split from Martin, later telling him that we'd been inside a school event in a hall. There were many chairs for the children's staged show and we sat down and watched, many parents attended. I felt out of place, not being a parent, but an event is an event, either be there or pass by. Upon the stage were kids dressed with ponytails and similar costumes, they were all girls and sang a Hindu song as they swayed their torsos left to right, I took a photo, thinking this great, unexpected fun to be at. Then a row of kids, younger, dressed in red filed on, danced around a bit and went off quickly, not doing the number of kids that had turned out for that act justice. There were not huge numbers of people watching, I thought this might be because a rehearsal was in progress, sadly, the event was only one tenth audience capacity. We allowed ourselves to be treated to this spectacle before returning out onto the street where it was back to the mundane reality of normal life, we mingled in the crowd, me feeling most lifted by the show.

We stopped regularly and talked to people, outside the chai shop was a common place for chit chat. I'd been communicating well in English with sign language, Katia had learned some Tamil, the local dialect, enough for a very limited conversation. She was learning new words all the time, eager to absorb them from people she talked with who were usually eager to teach. Often a conversation would involve surprise from the Indian that Katia could speak Tamil, and they would ask if she was fluent, she would reply in Tamil by saying she knew little. The delight that people showed was immense, Katia getting a lot out of the conversations she had. This she could keep up the whole day, while I tended to lose interest in having to make an effort all of the time, I found it tiring and the limited nature of the conversations not always worth pursuing.

I started to learn some Tamil and utilise a limited vocabulary of half a dozen words, finding I relied heavily upon English to get around. This was surprisingly easy, considering the distance I was from England, one of the benefits of the colonial repression that Britain had brought upon the area. I have learned more of the benefits brought to the area by colonialism, the transport and communications improvements, steam railways, telephones and roads were all speeded up by the presence of the British in India. I do not think the improvements were so necessary that blood should have been spilled over doing them, they would have happened anyway, eventually.

After another beautiful sunny day in Madurai, Katia and I had chatted with a person in the street and for free, we walked through an expensive shop on up to the rooftop. We were well above most roofs, overlooking the temple below us, the topmost parts of the towers still rising above us, I felt less daunted by them from up here. The inner courtyard of the temple was visible, people on the streets directly below, the street running straight along, moving people and machines far below. The roofs stretched out slightly below eye level, a mishmash of blue and yellow, the Brahmin painted theirs blue, other castes of lower status were other colours. Aerials rose above the roofs, clouds hung and drifted slowly, I lit a beedie and relaxed, Katia took photos, some of me, and we chatted together, having been joined also by a couple of tourists who had paid to be there!

Away from the bustling street there was peace, a different atmosphere. I relaxed a great deal, the day had been hard and my clothes were dirty from just being out and about, the dusty ground having risen up and blackened me. I didn't feel much like chatting with the people up the top but took to taking photos. Now, as the sun was setting, the scene took on a fleeting beauty of orangey, yellow light colouring the painted houses. The sun set behind the clouds as my camera clicked and did its stuff. The temple became more of a silhouette, the sun going behind, glinting out from the crescent summit of one tall gate side of the temple. The sun went as we watched, the lights of neon had been coming on, transforming the city. A sign of bright writing on bright background had some people around it with wooden poles, they were trying to fix something. The modern sight against the ancient temple was simple to capture, the bright light of the sign standing out against the dim, unlit twisty temple figures behind.

It was time to go down, our route did not take us through the shop, we had ended up alone on the roof. I thought that at least the memory of the moments up there have been captured on the camera, it was a want to share the tranquillity I found, to share it with the busy population below. At post dusk time, the streets were still full of traffic, the bustle never ending. I climbed up upon a metal box, one of those council ones at the side of a road and clicked at the glinting array of moving machines and the row of a hundred bicycles lined up on one side. We ate, drank and returned, becoming all the more good friends, and planning vaguely what we would do in the near future.

Chapter 34

The inevitable happened, we got off with each other, the age difference did not matter, we were attracted and that was natural. As Katia and I sat on the bed in her room, smoothly leaning on each other, becoming accustomed to our bodies being together, we kissed and kissed some more, embracing. We lay together kissing on the bed, my excitement brewing, but at the same time being happy just to kiss. I touched lightly her breast, a gentle stroke, hugging, touching her neck, she touched my neck sensually too, and I parted full of ecstasy. Out of the room I strode, not having unbuttoned her shirt, I felt like 'what am doing with her?' and at the same time 'wasn't it good?' I crept into bed, saying goodnight to the awake Martin who knew I had been at Katia's as my excitement gradually subsided and I slept. I told him the next morning, having thought more about the consequences of what had happened.

I could hardly believe the next day that I had been attracted to her and was a little repulsed by the thought that last night I had been so close with such an older woman, she was thirty five and I was nineteen, my mother was not much older. Love was off that day as I regretted what I'd done and was cold towards Katia who didn't take it too badly, giving me some space as we went, Martin me and her together for a morning excursion, she went somewhere else after lunch.

That evening Katia and I carefully watched a milk pourer, an event that we'd seen every day commonly, the great skill and the performance of making the chai was worth watching. We ordered chai from the stall we were at, also little sweet things to munch quickly. The tea was poured from a pot into cups, one being held in each hand, one hand down and one hand up as the chai came out of the pot, bubbling into the (usually) glass cup. The pot was filled from a large tank, kept under heat, the mixture of milk and tea and water reaching customers hotter if the pot had just been filled.

The pot periodically needed to be topped up from the main tank and the tea mixed, this was a spectacle. The milk in a metal jug was lifted in one hand and poured into the other, the pour starting off level and hands dropping and rising to make the milk bubble fiercely as it cascaded accurately into the lower one. The hands were then reversed in heights, stretching apart again and the jugs refilled back to how they were, this was repeated until the mix was right. In with the milk were cinnamon spices and other bits and pieces. Twenty pours might be what was needed to make the mix right before it was poured in the heated pot and served. I photoed a young lad doing it who emphasised the height difference between his hands until he could not stretch further apart. He smiled a lot, not spilling a drop and all around knew when the photo was taken as there was a flash. The crowd had liked the spectacle and we drank our drinks as the atmosphere died down to a happy and cosy mingling of hot chai sippers.

Chapter 35

The issue was now what to do next. Pete at Kovalam has said the most difficult thing to do was to decide which thing to have from the menu, I felt like that. Madurai was explored, museums and other more out of the way tourist attractions were not on our list. Katia and I decided to travel together, to Rameswaram, Martin was to visit many temples, cities, and wonderful places between here and, our meeting place. I did not want to trek along to lots of sights in a fashion that I took to be hurried but instead more enjoyed settling into one place. We were to split for ten days, it was okay as we knew where to meet - Mahabalipuram was the place and it wasn't that big. Martin was somewhat easy to identify, the tall English geezer with blond, curly hair and pale skin. It was arranged and we parted on our own paths which had been together through a lot so far.

We soon left for the Varanasi of the south, Rameswaram, a religious centre in southern India, a short boat ride away from Sri Lanka. I thought of popping over for a few days to have a taste of the island. Martin was to leave Maduri a day or two later and fixed himself up with a hotel single room, saving money. We parted with no great farewell. This was now me, travelling where and how I pleased, more so than before earlier in the trip. The freedom I felt in India was enormous and now it was greater still. With Katia as my easygoing companion, who needed no looking after (less than me anyway), I was out to see the world, having broken that last tie and connection with my friends, family and school, for a while at least.

At the station there was a little wait after our rickshaw ride, the luxury trip had left us with plenty of time, we sat and I chatted with a westerner about guidebooks, I showed him mine and he showed me his, mine was much better. I said that I'd seen them for sale for a fair price in Bombay, in the tourist stall street near to the low grade hotels. He left, "happy travelling" I said, and that was the last I shall ever probably see of him, I was used now to that happening, tuning in to the transitory nature my life had taken on, fleeting conversations one after another.

We train rode to Rameswaram, the excitement of being on the move again was good, the stuffiness of the city dispersed as the miles clocked up, sights out of the window were as always a pleasure to let pass by like a movie as the vehicle rolled along. Katia had a small amount of luggage, no rucksack but bags. This trip was in the night, we slept easily on separate bunks for the long dark haul, luxury class and so little was said to our fellow passengers. The train was crowded when I awoke early the next morning, people moving about, clamour made everyone who was not impervious to noise awake. I waited for a chai stop, as at the next station there would be some sold.

The loo was free, so into the smelly cubicle, standing peeing through the round hole onto the moving stones below the track. I could do with a hot drink. I thought, the water in the loo from the tap was probably okay, they filled it up regularly, it seemed okay, the water from my wet hands that I splashed onto my face was great. I got blown dry near to the window as I again sat in peace, now less bothered about the immediate absence of chai availability. Rather than a splash, I needed a bath for India is grimy, trains there are like the pavements of the city, the floors having a dusty layer from being a well trodden corridor. It was dawn, I had not brought a watch with me, though the camera did have the time on it, I very rarely needed to be at a place at a time.

The carriage door was wide open to the scenery outside the dark, dingy train. I stood looking at the slowly moving ground near to us, then beyond to the outlying countryside, a cyclist could have kept up with the speed we attained. I sat, beginning to enjoy the spectacle and in my dozy state I could do little else. With my feet resting on the ledge outside, a push and I'd be sprawling below, not the sort of rush the British Railways trains take, but then, they do get places faster. The sun rose, the air warmed and I tingled as the train ran into the day, the sitting gave me a chance to suss out the situation and plan ahead to consider what I was letting myself in for. I was free to do my own thing and that was just now to travel with Katia. I'd pretty much continually been with girlfriends since fifteen and felt close enough to Katia that we could hug each other in public places, this we did little, her independence outweighing mine. I thought about what Indians would think of my extremely old catch and reckoned that I'd gain a lot of respect.

The ground whirred by as I stood to check on Katia, asleep, she must have had earplugs, so back I went to the doorway and watched some more, feeling now independent, I had made it. I was a traveller and becoming accustomed to feeling laid back and cool for the vast majority of the time which most travellers seemed to do. They did not need drugs to do this, instead the effect of seeing loads of places and lifestyles at first hand enhanced their street credibility to such an extent that they were categorically cool and knew a great deal, were never heavy but very easy going.

I spent so little time thinking of my family, friends and other relations, the people around me now were those who mattered most. I had not put pen to paper for anyone since the first train journey on days one and two. No phone calls did I make, Martin did and I thought about doing so too, but the expense and the technicalities of doing it had not appealed, so no one at home knew my movements. They of course had the chance to think about what I was doing and so probably guessed a bit, they had not heard from the British embassy that I was dead so at least they knew I was alive or at least most likely to be.

I didn't try to suss out the buffet car, the trip to the loo was as far as I wanted to go along the now wide awake bustling train, except for a sleepy chap in our segment of carriage. This was the first class area of the train, further along, the passengers had been sleeping where they sat, we had taken the easy option this journey and anyway I wanted to be with Katia as we accompanied each other. She rose, not having changed any clothes or taken them off to sleep either, the next stop was the town of our destination.

Chapter 36

We alighted, goods gathered along with us heading quickly for a chai shop and breakfast stop, sitting with the bags outside, I thumbed vaguely through the guidebook. We were to head to the temple, it sounded nice, this was a very holy town after all. We just had to find a hotel, that was easy, we picked one the guide book said was of medium price. It was clean, cool, ventilated, lacking visibly in airborne insects, we took a double room. The journey naturally had been tiring and I felt like resting but Katia thought I had the wrong idea so we went walking as the day was beginning to heat up. Our hotel was close by where sea shells were for sale in stalls. Strung in necklaces, strings of beautiful shells all of the same type. They had been plundered, probably remorselessly, from the sea in the area, or else had been brought in, for selling to pilgrims.

There were few westerners here, the town had lost popularity among travellers as the ferry to Sri Lanka didn't run due to war troubles in the area. Later we spoke with a local fisherman who said that we could pay someone to do a trip, it was possible to get to the island, although I thought it an idea worth dropping knowing of the war problems there. The trip was out then, he did cheer us up however by giving us a tot of rum and inviting us casually to a card game, with gambling that was due to run later in the week, in the evening. I liked being invited, I remembered his name and quite fancied gambling, not having done any before. We pressed on, me saying to Katia that I thought a card game gambling with real money seemed quite daring, he did seem quite rich and could probably afford to lose a little. Katia too was invited to this men's gathering, I thought that was a good thing, something you can get away with, just from being a westerner.

If you are a western traveller then, along with some of the inhuman emotions thrown at you, like beggars trying harder, people hard-selling and some disapproving looks, there are also bonuses. This is because you have such a free lifestyle, and become used to going anywhere and doing what you want. The Indians pick up on that and invite you to do things, even though their own wives and friends would not partake in such ritual. Perhaps he said it to humour me, he was nice though, later in the week was fine, no get your money out now, no pressure, if you feel like it later on sort of thing. We left the fat businessman of a fisherman sitting on some wood in the night air, sipping his expensive drink and walked on, looking around us and talking deeply about our experiences that we were having at that moment. We walked slowly, unhurriedly back to the hotel where we undressed and slept, no sex, the comfort of being in bed with another person was what I needed most at that time, that was enough.

Chapter 37

Scoring was on the agenda, we'd run out of grass and wanted to get high together. The steps of the hotel led onto the roof and from this flat spacious verandah I could see the temple and nearly to the sea beyond. Over the roofs were we, in our private space above all the rest, free to indulge in our silly fantasies and do exciting things. The grass scene was not happening, but more underground here because there were less travellers, things were harder. I asked the hotel boy who had said he could sort us out with anything, I said "yes please" and I said I'd give him the money when I saw the stuff. That afternoon we took siesta, skipping the bothersome heat of the day, I searched out my hotel boy who was not around. I returned upstairs to bed in the cool room where the fan turned round and Katia lay in the dress code for cooling, wrapped with the sheet from the bed.

In the evening I again chased the hotel boy and was pleased with him, he had accomplished his mission with a little bit of grass around five rupees worth, enough for a few days. He got many thanks from me. I did not worry about police as the amount involved was so small and anyway who is going to bother to bother someone for enjoying themselves. As I got over feeling powerful that I could implement an illegal thing I triumphantly went upstairs to Katia, I quickly started taking apart a beedie to fill it with grass, before curling the leaf back up again with the substance enclosed to smoke it. The beedies were proving a problem as they were so dry, unrolling the outer leaves caused extensive cracking that made the thing break up. By the third one I had a damaged but smokable item, I showed it off to Katia, joking about my terrible spliff making ability, and lit the thing pulling hard, anxious to get high. After just a few puffs the thing went out and was bandaged up, I got the hang of doing it after trying more and found another way without papers. I had seen a guy crumble out a cigarette into the palm of his hand, throw half of the tobacco on the ground, add half grass mixing with his thumb pressing in the palm of his hand. Then curled his palm to channel and pour in the herbs to the empty cigarette with the filter in the end. He did this very quickly and smoothly, when I first tried it, the tobacco was too stuck together and damp to get out of the cigarette.

The fact that Katia smoked was cool, she had travelled over to the other side of the world, a female alone, strong and independent. She was having some time off to travel and think, before financing herself further by working again, writing and taking photos. She had it sussed and good luck to her, she could (and was) doing anything she liked. I reckoned that she was an influence on some of the more oppressed women in India and that passing through an area, having women staring at her, so sexy, and showy, and sure of herself, must have been a morale boost to them that women really can do this. Katia was full of respect as well towards the people she was living among, as was I. That brought us together, having a great deal in common, wanting to achieve the same thing by simply being in India. Living among the people there as one of them, and not feeling apart from the community, but integrating along with it. We were both into people, we'd talk a lot with anyone, whoever we met in the street, being unbiased and full of life energy, bright eyed, enthusiastic, on the go. This need to feel normal among people with whom we were unfamiliar was what kept us together, our shared deep perception meant that we treated folk like ordinary everyday people, chatting in a casual way.

At last the tourist mould was breaking for me, that state of mind when one rushes through a potentially pleasurable holiday, not enjoying it on account of hurrying about too much and not realising that haste is the reason it was not being enjoyed. Our understanding of each other grew, empathy increasing, our being on the same high, smoking often, with a bong made out of a plastic bottle, bubbling smoke through water before sucking it in our mouths. A similar drug going through our systems in large quantities bent us each apart from our normal lines of comprehension of the world. We, together, let ourselves be altered by the drug and in so doing saw the world with new eyes. Our communication grew from deep conversation into knowing each other's state of mind, and anticipating needs before they became verbalised.

Chapter 38

On a few consecutive nights we heard a distressed donkey running in the streets of Rameswaram, it ran along all around the town in the night, clearly audible from our rooftop position. We thought that it may have lost a child, panicking in its desperate search through the town. Made a hell of a din, the harsh donkey cry repeated in a desperate attempt to call out, but with no reply. It became hoarser, and as it ran around, the energy within it was being used up, it was becoming exhausted. We heard it a second night, it had been joined by another four legged beast and together they trotted around the town, the donkey still crying out. Then, a third night of distress, with less calls, it did not lose its voice as I would have done but had become worn out, eventually giving up the search, so by the fourth night it was silent again in the town, the sounds of despair and desperation had quietened.

Perhaps someone had put a stop to the thing by killing it and putting it out of the misery it was facing, or perhaps it was too valuable to kill so the owner had let it get over its trauma in this way before taking it in again, under their wing. Another different day I noticed that all the dogs in town had been culled, they were all about the town with their heads buried in sand, dead. I looked at one for a long while, thinking about its innocence, then the next day they were all gone and I wondered if I had actually seen them.

We spent the days strolling through the town, meeting the folk, sometimes together, sometimes alone, we both liked the main temple, it was a place of peace nearby to the sea. Each morning the pilgrims underwent a thorough half hour of worship, before continuing with their day. Katia, a regular early riser, was into photographing the spectacle that she had learned about and I came along with her. The morning routine for the travelled worshippers consisted of a soaking with a measure of water from each of the wells of the temple and one from the central pool. They ran or walked onto the next one along the connecting paths, we watched the event, walking along the paths, not fancying getting soaked. We skipped the queues for a dowsing, letting the soaked runners file past us. Katia loved the energy and enthusiasm in this morning ritual, it was dawn time, the day far from hot. I wondered if the pilgrims continued wearing the sodden clothes or if they went home for breakfast and a change, and also, I wondered what was organised for them in the daytime.

Katia took photos, I felt this was a liberty, to modernise this respected, sacred ritual, but I sometimes had silly feelings like that, not realising that by taking the photos, the ritual was not being spoilt in anyway. Stepping out of the temple, the sun was low, the day just warming, we were awake, so much of the day was still ours to enjoy, we went to the beach. There people swam clothed, it seemed the best way to swim, that is what everybody else did, taking off only my sandals, I swam. The shorts and t-shirt quickly drying, my thin clothes proving little discomfort to endure whilst they dried on me, I beckoned to Katia to join me, she was not interested. On the beach and in the water was quite a gathering of people, I imagined they were all drawn to this place of worship. A man had built a sandcastle and put on it bits of shiny metal, little scraps as decoration and people coming up to him made an offering to him, in return for which they were blessed. Why did they give this guy their money for a pathetic sand castle is what I wondered, godliness growing inside them must have been the motive for such a purchase, a good return on their investment they thought.

This was a fresh day, I'd risen before quite a few people, compared to usual, though many busy folk were certainly already up and going much earlier, and used to doing so most days of their lives. We ate cooked bread stuff and I polished the lot off as usual, leaving a clear plate and asked Katia if she was going to finish hers. She said no and ordered chai, I thought she was being a waster, leaving food on her plate in a country with such poverty. I thought it wrong of her, briefly discussing this with her, it got my back up a bit as she was doing something that I thought so senseless.

Another time I went into a shop with carvings, chessboards

with amazing pieces, ornate mirrors and antique furniture. An expensive sort of shop, but curiosity about the elephants and other elaborate chess pieces in the window interested me. I saw, on the wall, a wooden carving of a pop-eyed monster, tongue lolling out, a face of chaos, I stared at it for a while. On subsequent days I came back twice more just to look at this scary, chaotic forces of nature face. It seemed almost real, unlike any of the other items. I kept thinking about it then decided, most unusually for me, to buy this expensive item as it was simply calling out to me by appearing so real and alive. This heavy, expensive, impractical to carry, large wooden face kept me company on the trip and I have it still. I was so drawn to it, perhaps the same chaotic forces of the face were churning inside of me. A picture of my emotions and inner world made tangible on a colourful, intricate piece of wood. So unusual, so filled with meaning that I wanted it near me, to physically have possession of something that so struck a chord with my emotions.

Chapter 39

I was to score some more grass today, our supply having almost disappeared. In the town was a bunch of young lads whom I recognised quite well, having had a few chats and a smoke together. I met one lad, finding out he and his mate were going to a temple just out of town, I went with them. Sitting peacefully in the cool, I chatted to a man there, he said that I could buy some high quality material silks etc. and take them over to the other side of India, in the direction from which I had come and earn myself some money acting as a courier. I said that I thought I liked the sound of the idea but I did not dare to trust the man, as selling two hundred pounds worth of his goods to me and sending me off a few hundred miles away seemed to me that he was at little risk of losing out on the deal. I also did not have any idea about what the prices were of the material in the markets either this side or the other side of India. I declined, even while he assured me that plenty of other westerners had tried out being a courier with him and he had had no complaints. He was strongly persuasive but I gently refused. The other guys whom I was there with were perhaps embarrassed that they had brought along this guy (me) who was refusing to take up the man's extremely generous offer, the fact I had the money meant that I could. To the younger lads, this guy with the fabric seemed like a father, the younger guys poor, having little opportunity to do things with their lives. I felt that perhaps they thought of me as an arrogant young westerner, who knew better than the lot of them, and thought himself wiser.

Then he started talking about me getting a wife, because I liked India so much, I could, if I was married, return at will to the country, having few visa problems. He said that he knew how he could get me one and that I could return to India at any time and stay for as long as I liked. I assured him I had no desire to marry anyone, startled at the idea of it being so easy to marry a woman here, having an ever faithful servant, with whom you could communicate only ineffectively and probably lose interest in after a while. I thought that her interest in me would be difficult to comprehend and that she would be like cattle to accept such an offer from a stranger, there was no way I could go through with it.

The conversation ended with me feeling strained at keeping up my manners although we parted company gentlemen, he went. The group of us left there in the temple proceed to chat with each other, not talking about the man much, and rolling up some grass and smoking it. I had my camera and took a few weird shots with it of the inside of the empty steps area around the central pool in the centre of a courtyard area in the temple. Two young boys swam in the murky lake and I photographed them as well, walking away from the group of lads to do this.

The conversation turned to that of a sexual nature, prompted by the man before. I took it very easy, believing extremely restrictive sexual beliefs in India existed. These boys had surely not seen much action nor would expect to see much compared with what a westerner could reasonably expect to see by my age. I did not go into details but said that I had had the usual western experiences, they asked me how old I was. I did not say that I had been having sex fairly continually with a range of different girls since sixteen as, in comparison to them, I felt like a prostitute, the cheap nature of sex having been revealed to me. I thought of sex as an easy thing to get, an important thing, one that I should get as much of as possible. I had little urge in India, at last finding something more to occupy me.

I was becoming wiser, more experienced at everyday matters and my perspective on life was broadening to wider horizons. The Indian based religion, Hinduism, believes in karma, this I thought about quite a bit. Karma is similar to how much you have in a spiritual bank account, the accumulation of good deeds to your fellow man and to life on Planet Earth. The result of the karma you had was expressed in your position relative to other people on earth and the areas in which you lived and worked. My understanding of this way of thinking grew in India, the more spiritual good you did, the better position you would find yourself in life.

I went away from the temple and read a little in the afternoon, relaxed, showered and dozed away. I thought about what other travellers had in their rucksacks or bags and how much that said about someone's personality and priorities in life, from what they decided to carry around with them on a long backpacking trip.

Chapter 40

Once we went and changed rupees into ten paise pieces, getting nine of them at the nearby stall and moving along a line of incredible elderly holy men giving them out. There were about forty of them stood in a row, each with wrinkles, shabby clothes and wisdom beyond measure. Part of me wanted to give them everything I had as they were more worthy then me, what an amazing example of humanity they made. They had chosen this life and giving in this way was part of what made the world go round so I joined in the ritual, being blessed from my giving to them. I felt awestruck, honoured and humbled at these superior men, Katia took it as much more of a fun thing to do, smiling at each one as she gave, so much less serious than I was.

We walked a little at night here, Katia and I went around in the cool air looking at the town at this very different time of day. Outside of the temple walls were huge stones, rectangular in shape, as yet unpositioned. Upon them were bodies, men asleep in everyday clothes, draped on these rocks. Stalls were all closed, few people were up doing things, we walked in the contrasting stillness, looking around at the darkened, silent town. One chai shop was the place to be, a gathering always, the people working there did so till late at night, we chatted and partied on down, I smoked beedies. That shop was the nearest shop to the hotel which had any activity at night, walking all the way around the temple, we found it was the only place that had something to offer. As the night was cool we stayed out in it quite often, getting to know the shop and feeling at ease there as more people got to know the pair of us.

This night time expedition habit led me to be sitting on a wooden hand cart parked on a street, chatting with a small group of westerners, Europeans some of them were, the conversation became lively. I was smoking beedies, lit with matches, as lighters made an expensive investment in comparison. An old man walked up to us, with a stick in his hand, he grabbed all of our attention. He asked us a question, "If man sends machines up into space what will space think there is on earth?" We discussed this point for a little while, I enjoyed talking to him, others in the group tuned their attention to other things.

I kept up the conversation because, to hear this old man dressed in a blue turban and simple dress, talking of outer space was unexpected and interesting. Science and him surely were not linked, but he posed an interesting insight into the possible misunderstanding of man's efforts to communicate with aliens. I said that pictures had been made and attached to probes, history chronicled in a new language that aliens might be able to understand, so how could they not know what was here on earth? All they had to do was understand and decipher our messages to them. I think the man was saying that humans should go up themselves to communicate with aliens or else there could be some misunderstanding. Perhaps, I thought, if the misunderstanding was large enough, then we could be creating our own end to the planet being overtaken by a superior force that we had annoyed, unwittingly and unintentionally. He passed on and I knew that I wanted to see him again, Rameswaram was not that large a place after all.

Chapter 41

We listened to music sometimes on Katia's Walkman, with built in speakers and microphone. She did not have much in the way of tapes but played one of talking and guitar playing with a discordant recorder over it, a funky discord recorder, out of touch in some way with the rest of the musicians, but complementing the tune overall, tuneful for sure. Katia told me the recording had been made on top of the mountain at John's place, when I first met her. She had pushed record and plonked the machine in the room, picking up Martin's' guitar efforts with me making that extraordinary sound with the recorder. I realised I sounded like a sixties spaced out, psychedelic player. I did think I was quite good and could hardly believe that it was me and not a professional of some sort.

One evening we went to the beach, Katia showed me the purse of condoms she had with her, we walked down to the water's edge in the evening cool and lay down. I had fascinations that we would be making love under the moon on the beach, it didn't happen though, I was too inhibited. We lay and sat for a while, and calmly and slowly made our way back to the hotel. The moonlight on the barely moving water, the sand, the quiet, and lack of human company around made this another getaway place in the near proximity of the town. I didn't even kiss her on that beach then but spoke instead with her about what she did and who she was in life. From Canada, French speaking, working as a journalist, having been on the unending road now for a couple of years, working as she went. Katia was married to a guy in Canada. This I couldn't digest, why then, was she away from him and more to the point, why was she showing an interest in me? That was breaking a very big rule surely. I still couldn't get comfortable with the age difference or the marriage status, but we were friends.

Later I talked some more regarding her husband, he is a very liberal husband she assured me, so that was cleared up. I felt much better for the fact that the husband involved had more of less given his consent to the actions which were taking place, over on the other side of the world where he could do little about them anyway. Still it was good to know that at least we were not breaking any rules in that nobody actually minded us being with each other sexually. Breaking the standardised rules in this way gave me some thrill, it was so very much against my usual way of thinking, just so absolutely laidback, without hassle.

I had left a girlfriend back in London, Reau, we also had a liberal relationship, agreeing that while I was away that I'd see how it went and she'd do too. There were no rules between us about faithfulness, instead, to take things as they came, and as they happened. I told Katia of Reau and the arrangement we had just so she did not feel bad she may have been breaking anyone's heart whilst I went out with her. To be on the road for a couple of years, going all over the world is an unusual way to be. I imagine that Katia could choose anywhere in the world to go and go there, writing articles on the way, earning enough to perpetuate the movement she had.

Katia had brought along some clay-like soil which was soap, the grime when rubbed took off a great deal of dirt and grease. This was funny to us that you should have to get so dirty to become clean, we covered our faces and I took photos in the shower of the hotel room. I did not care so much about becoming clean, spreading mucky clay all over me was much better fun. Katia painted tribal marks in the mud with her wet finger, the laughter was captured on the camera. She wanted to make love with me, I was still so unsure about it. She asked me if it was because she had birthmarks on her body, I said of course that was nothing to do with it. She felt rejected and I then consented and we had our only, brief, sexual encounter with each other, remaining friends but not lovers.

Chapter 42

The relationship was sometimes a trifle intense in the realm of psychic activity, some of the things that happened took me and her by surprise, freaking us out a bit. One evening, on top of the roof, we sat and pulled from the bong, which was now part and parcel of our hotel room equipment. I was becoming quite stoned. I played about on the roof, running round and round in circles, becoming dizzy and turning around to run the other way in an attempt to undizzy myself. My feet slapped barely upon the tarmac roof as I ran dementedly, enjoying myself that I was being so stupid and silly in the company of a cool adult who didn't mind what I was up to.

There was some clamour in the street below, out the front of the hotel, I was toward the other end of the roof when Katia looked over the edge of the low wall at the scene, she thought of taking a photo. I came up to her soon afterwards and said I'd had a flash in my mind of a calf amid a throng of people, being pulled and stretched among them. In the street below was the scene which I had pictured, a throng of people with a calf in the middle, in my mind the calf had been on its side, now, in the street it was upright.

Katia said that her intensified interest in the scene had projected the image that she saw to me. I imagined that was why she was a photographer, I hope she did not do that to people too often, taking photos perhaps being safer. I did think, however, the experience was one to be savoured, I had never had such an intense, close relationship with a person in this way. The fact of communication becoming easy, with no words, meant we were bonding closer, in tune with one another.

Downstairs in the hotel room we tried again to do more forced and less spontaneous psychic communication. I looked intensely at something while Katia tried to suss what I was looking at. She did to an extent, the vague shape of the grilled window reached her mind, we'd done it. This was actually a way of communicating with other people without having necessarily to talk to them. Something so new to me, I found it very exciting, and believed I processed great psychic power. I believed that I was quite a magical person who had known very well that I could do all this before, but now, having proved it so completely, I felt I had become a master at this realm of communication. The confidence I felt with myself was enormous, I could do anything now surely, if the usual borders of communication had been crossed, the world was unlimited. I could nip into minds at will and do things that nobody guessed I was doing, as they would be so unconventional compared to what people normally expected. Wow! What spice had been added to my life that rooftop evening. It was as if I had discovered a new ability that had lain dormant, I had become aware of more of me, the energy I felt was extraordinary.

Chapter 43

I looked at the sun, it was around noon, high in the sky, little ground shadow. I looked at the sun, straight at it, without blinking, squinting my eyes, straight at that globe of fire, that huge nothingness ball which is so definitely there, making its presence felt. Usually common sense would warn me away from this foolish act for fear of damaging my eyesight, but I continued to look. I just saw, just nothingness there, burning up, containing nothing though it was all the energy which made my life possible. It is nice to know about where things come from, and looking at the sun helped me to understand a great deal. I felt spiritually prepared to do this and viewed the spectacle with great patience, trying to gain as much information in as short a time as possible, it being a dangerous thing to do for too long. An empty sphere of pure energy, a sun that had been worshipped for centuries. I didn't think it special, just there it was. Returning my sight to the earthly surroundings, I was back in the world that I was used to.

I met the philosopher man again, it was on the street on an off-chance, as I'd been hoping. I was on a bicycle and said to him that I had to dash off to the shop before my charge for the bicycle doubled as the hour went into two hours. I agreed to take a few minutes to talk with him and together we spoke. He was great, and totally calmed me down, we chatted a bit about space. I tried to give him as much information as I could, knowing far more than he about the current ins and outs of space technology and exploration. The topics diverged, I said I was from England, that my grandparents had been in India for a while. He asked me if we could walk into the shade and have a chai, I told him about the cycle place, then decided that it didn't matter much, going with him to the chai shop, he bought me one. I hung around, feeling the strong spirituality of this man close by to me, his effect was magical, he blended in with his surroundings well. We talked and soon I left, having found out vaguely whereabouts he lived, cycling calmly and serenely to the cycle shop for which I did not have to pay extra.

Now, knowing his location, I could find him easily, at my leisure. I cycled down the road out of town along a road flanked by the sea, sparse vegetation on each side, rocks, cacti sort of plants which I stopped at to look at on the way back. He was around and we started to chat, I had a great deal which I wanted to say to him. He patiently kept telling me that there was no need for me to rush and that I should slow down a bit and take things easy, even try to enjoy myself a bit by absorbing the beauty of the moment. My enthusiasm was high and I was to learn a lot from this guy, as a willing pupil. We drank tea, smoked a touch of grass, we watched the sun in the sky at the end of the day and wandered along the beach near to the worshippers absorbing the atmosphere, whilst being very much independent of it, tuning more into our own senses.

Looking at the sunset that evening, the oranges of the sky slowly changing, the colours never the same twice, he told me to look at the different variations: "Look at the orange, at the yellow, at the blue above, the different stripes of colour across the sky." On examination of the whole by its independent bits, a focus was achieved. The concentration on these bits helping me to put them together to form an overall picture of reality that was really in depth and made me appreciate what I saw that little bit more.

He was into living in the moment, a tingling, lively, sparkling old man, he'd been experiencing reality to the full more that most people had been fortunate enough to do. This was then what I had to aim for, to live in the moment, to feel excited and appreciate the boundlessness of the beauty of nature to the full as often as I could. In a few moments of experiencing nature this way, it felt like years of schoolroom teaching absorbed, so intense was the experience that I was never the same again. It was like reading the entire works of Shakespeare in a second and consuming it all.

On walking around near to the temple I felt an extreme sense of peace and began to tune into what he was saying regarding the power of this holy place and how it kept on pulling people towards it. For centuries worship had happened there, he said that energy was coming out of the earth and being absorbed by the pilgrims in this holy place. I imagined people taking the energy, attracted as pilgrims here, not knowing they were taking something vital from the earth. I started imagining that a wound existed, too much had been taken, an imbalance that might cause a catastrophe. I thought more, about a huge sleeping dragon, the pilgrims washing in the water, wading through the smoke of the dragon, pacifying it and keeping it asleep, and continuing to take the energy. More effort was needed to pacify the beast the greater the imbalance of earth energy. This needed plenty of wise old men around, keeping the peace, an ancient effort I was witness to and pupil of.

Chapter 44

Gandhi had his ways of pacifistic peacekeeping, here the peacekeepers were recognised by the holy status of their clothes and coloured powder on their foreheads. They smiled but the battle was tough, especially so if sex had not been a feature for so long, because to be a holy man is to withdraw from the pleasures of sex. Perhaps the overindulgence in pleasure that I had been a part of could in some way be balanced out by being near to these holy men. I almost felt unclean compared to them, I believed that in their eyes I was unwashed.

I was changing, Katia and myself never really hit it off sexually, I had given it a go but found that I was not interested, very unusually for me. I was getting into something higher, which at that time sex was in the way of. My speedy spiritual development could not falter purely for the sake of indulging in the bodily pleasures of life. I had already done so with many girlfriends, I felt I was already an insult to the practice of chastity. In order that I learnt fast, my pleasure was kept to smoking marijuana, tobacco and of course drinking chai. With these three drugs seeing to my greedy needs, I felt balanced out for a lesson in spirituality which I was so keen to take on and learn.

I believed marijuana to be a shortcut to some kind of shadow of spiritual enlightenment and this was encouraged by the philosopher man. At the same time, he cleverly educated me in focusing on what I really wanted. This was my own spiritual development, to get my own concentration going, to wake up and consciously take part in life on a spiritual level.

An exciting prospect, he told me that "one day you may be a judge", seeing great potential in my future, I might have to make important decisions by myself that might effect the future of the world. I needed someone extremely wise to guide me, wiser than the teachers at school, wiser than my parents with their accumulated life experience. I needed this old man, who was practically a tramp, and his wisdom. He in turn knew what I was after, and tried to lead me along a little and help me to see things for myself, to be in the moment. Higher than this chap could only be God, for this man was independent from the hordes of holy men, he was really special and knew the score, my personal priest, who happened to be into what I was into and never asked for anything, but loved to teach. I was led, a little innocently and gently, into something very much bigger by a stranger who would not tell me his name, or where he was from, as it didn't matter. I knew I wanted to go beyond the ordinary, to immerse myself in the unknown and to break the bonds and constraints of everydayness which I had become used to at school and in my life so far, stepping out was now what I was about.

Chapter 45

Katia and I had been getting on fine but she did not like the way I was regularly off with this man, getting into what she was not. She didn't relate well to what it was I was doing, I told her that this was really important to me and that it was not going to stop. I knew in the back of my mind I had a date to meet with Martin, I was determined to stick to it, despite having to shorten my maximum time in Rameswaram to ten days. Inevitably the day did arrive, my backpack packed I set out to catch a taxi, I had said goodbye to my guru and said goodbye to Katia. I sensed so strongly her sadness as I departed, she hung out of a window upstairs in the hotel and waved, I walked on after waving goodbye, not looking back again, trying to clear the sadness emanating from her out of my mind.

I found a taxi and headed into town for the train station, I was a little nervous at travelling so far alone, half of that came out as excitement though. I made it to the town area with ease, sorted out things at the station regarding tickets and times and had a little time to wait until I was on my way on the train to Madras. The voyage out from Rameswaram went over a metal railway bridge on the steaming train, the water ran out on the tidal rip as the train passed over the flowing water. The whole world seemed strange, the power of the water rushing below was tremendous, the flowing surface was moving beneath in a different direction to that of the train. Recovering from feeling unsure about the relatively narrow concrete supporting posts in comparison to the flood, I enjoyed the strange feeling, knowing the low likelihood of a major catastrophe.

I sat as a lone westerner here in the carriage, I saw the journey through without talking much, dozing off a bit. I was very much alone and that suited me, just looking out of the window now and then, not making much of an effort to talk. Although good conversation could have happened between the people there and myself, I did not feel up to it. Along the way, the steam train stopped for water, drinking from a railway side, holding up the journey for everyone. I expected the trip to be totally different as this was a steam train but it wasn't, other than knowing we were all being pulled by an old steam engine.

Chapter 46

On arrival at Madras (now Chennai) I walked up to the front of my Rameswaram train, said a few words of thanks to the steam train crew who had been working hard. I felt a little like an old fashioned English gentleman doing this deed. I needed lunch and took a short rickshaw ride to a cafe but left my shoes in it, a lucky person would probably pick them up, perhaps without the driver knowing. They were a good pair, made from old car tires and leather, by a small outfit consisting of old men sitting on the floor in a little wooden shack, they had been reasonably priced and promised to be long lasting, certainly a lucky find.

I dropped into a grotty looking, basic, chip shop equivalent food place, serving low class grub. It was what I needed, I was feeling very tired. I ate and drank, paid for the food, washing my hands after the meal where everyone else did, in a sink to the side, I still had to ask about the loo. I felt a little scruffy, unclean and disrespectful towards the Indians whose country I was visiting. I certainly had the finances to smarten myself up but I didn't care much as I was on a direct route to the station to take me away. I decided to leave for the other train station where the railway took me along northwards towards Mahabalipuram. Having made absolutely sure that I was on the right path, all I had to do was to mentally say goodbye to the cafe, thankful that there are such places for weary people like me. The place in itself was unappealing, the waiters were all young kids who I felt were probably overworked, and the company I think mostly regulars who seemed a bit put out at grubby me, adding to the self consciousness that I was feeling. I had not thought about the distance between the two train stations in Madras, this was quite a bit of a journey, unknown to me, I decided to walk my way to the connection station.

I was glad to go from the cafe as I pressed on ever into the new sights and sounds of grubby Madras, hauling the bag again onto my back and shuffling off toward the station barefooted but refreshed. The city was filled with dirt and an off smell of rubbish and sewage, the grime left from constant use of the area by so many people was making me dirtier and dirtier. My feet were holding up fine with little in the way of glass on the pavement. I looked down onto what I was standing on, but not very carefully, believing I would be safe in all but a few areas. Hundreds of people walked along these streets in bare feet, but they all had beggar status, I did not have that being a westerner so I must have seemed a little weird to the everyday folk there.

The road went on as did I, eventually making a further stop for some sugar cane juice sold at a little stall, I'd not tried it. It was good sweet liquid, better by far than Lucozade as the sugary stuff was natural, crushed in the hand driven machine in front of my eyes. I knew just what it contained, the couple there were nice, with kids probably, they allowed me to take a photo of the stall which came out badly but showed well the idea of the pram-like mobile stall complete with sugar cane crushing machine on top with the loving owners.

Further along there was a rickshaw stand with lots of friendly young men hanging about waiting for custom, I got chatting with them, they were a good laugh and before long we ended up in the back of one of the rickshaws having a joint. A friendly policeman came and joined in the banter and took position in the back of the rickshaw with me and one of the guys, chatting and sharing the joint before continuing on his way. I had thought that the situation might have been a set up as I would have been all too happy to have paid off the policeman rather than risk arrest but I trusted these young men and thankfully my instincts proved right. I soon continued on my way, energised with the sugar cane and peacefully hazy with the joint, uplifted by some good company, feeling rather cool that I had smoked with a policeman on duty.

Chapter 47

I met a guy near the station who said that he could score some Thai sticks and that a friend of his was in Mahabalipuram and I could pick them up at a hotel which he gave me the name of as well as the person whom I was to contact there. We went in a rickshaw (I paid) to head to the dealer who could be of help, unfortunately we did not meet up with him and had a rather wasted journey. The man was not disheartened and suggested that if I gave him fifty rupees that he would fix everything up for me in Mahabalipuram. I believed I was paying a good price so I exchanged money with him. He walked off with my money and he said that he would now walk toward where his friend was, as he thought he knew where he might be. I declined following him as the train was going to leave soon from the station and I would certainly miss it if I waited in Madras any longer. So off he walked across the road away from me, confidently, the money in his hand.

It was at that moment, I realised, I was never going to see any Thai sticks and that the man had been clever enough to make me part with the cash with his talk. There was no time for regrets, just about turn, rickshaw again, there were plenty, back to the station, my loss was not too bad, I thought, in the back of the rickshaw. I felt a little prince-like riding alone in the back of this chauffeur driven vehicle, it was so easy to get back to the station, and not one rickshaw had seemed to pass me when I walked earlier. I did not really know what I was missing out with regarding the Thai sticks, they were, I believed specially prepared Thai grass tied into sticks, the purity of the grass was capable of giving a high much sought after.

I managed to get to the station and onto a train for a long haul, the journey was through the night, I would be arriving the next morning assuming no disasters. I snuggled in, again not feeling much like talking to people, I had the beginning of diarrhoea. I was concentrating mostly on looking after myself for now, not having the effort to care about the people around me much, though I was aware of them. Supper, train motion, trips to the hole in the floor, looking at the railway sleepers passing, my poo becoming increasingly liquid-like and yellowish, falling on the moving tracks below. The main tank providing water to loo users had run dry, so pulling up my clothes I returned to the seat, a might squidgy between the cheeks. I still went barefoot, the surface of the train had a dusty and smooth, worn feel to it, an old feeling that gave me a sensation as though I was moving but rooted to the ground. I struggled to sleep on the rumbling train, people all around were very respectful about keeping quiet and letting everyone sleep, the babies and children around did so too.

This was a second class journey, my pack was above in the luggage rack, but I could not hope to make a bed there as other passengers had filled it up. The evening drew well into the night before I drifted off, surrounded closely with Indians only. I slept lightly, thinking vaguely about the bag and its value to someone crafty, vowing to wake up if the train stopped as it often did for inexplicable reasons during the night. Dawn came and the noise level started to rise, waking me, everyone else followed suit, getting ready so that shortly the trainload of people were ready for the first stop that occurred after dawn.

I thought to myself, as I wandered to an open door to look and feel the air, that I really fancied a cup of chai, just now it was what I most wanted in the whole world, there was none, nor a chap to serve it to the passengers. That we had to wait for, the next stop being an hour away, where breakfast and chai would be readily available at the bustling station. It was dawn, the sun was coming up on the right of the train, I found a doorway open, a wooden step beneath, I sat, resting my feet and legs in the cool air. We moved slowly, I thought I might have been able to run as fast, not that I felt like it, I was still weak from being sick out of my arse. The sun slowly lifted, the day beginning, I was actually beating the farmers and villagers up and was going already! I thought to myself about what was going on, settled doubts largely, and accepted that I must be doing the right thing or else I would not be doing it. After ten hours of night time cool, half an hour was all it needed for the heat to start, the area was easy to heat up, on account of the land being so dry.

Chapter 48

I was at peace with the beautiful world then, uncaring of how ill I felt, or that I did not quite know the whereabouts of Martin. I didn't mind that I was being ripped away from what I wanted to do, I had been in the middle of something quite good when leaving Rameswaram, learning to rise above the humdrum of everyday existence to new spiritual heights. The best thing was to go Indian style and take the whole happening as fate and for the best, that anything happening is the will of the Gods and perfectly right. This is nice on many levels, for example, it favours a lack of shoving in queues and other patient niceties. But fatalism can become too extreme, for example when you start thinking that working for a bastard of a boss is fate and you accept this version of slavery. It was happening all over India, a lot of people working very hard and a few rich big wigs keeping the show rolling in the direction most suited to them.

The cup of chai was absolutely worth every second I had to wait for it, delicious, warm, a touch of cinnamon, I decided against breakfast in style and had myself just a few mouthfuls of food. My stomach hurt, and I was feeling weak, that I was ill, I was sure but I didn't worry about it as there was little that I could do until I got off the bloody train and slept a bit, recovering from it all. I managed to get off at the right stop, walked to the front and viewed the impressive diesel engine, saying thank you to the driver. I made my way to town, an easy enough task. I had the feeling that there was an off chance of Martin being there to welcome me, I hoped for this as it's nice to be welcomed to a place, but there was no one waiting for me, so I walked on.

Dumping the bag was something I wanted to do. In the growing heat, I asked people of Martin's whereabouts and got to know that he had recently moved, this delayed things a little, the fact he was out when I arrived was no problem. I chatted with his new landlords, explaining my predicament, found a bed outside in the shade and crashed, trusting my bag in their hands. I felt awful after expelling more yellow liquid, at least able this time to wipe myself using the standard left hand and water method. The landlady woman there was worried but I said that I was okay, all would be alright, the biggest thing on my mind was a kip before Martin showed. I told a westerner there of my intentions and he said that the message would be passed on if he saw Martin. I thanked him and also the landlady for her kindness and rested, gently falling into the depth of sleep, I realised, lying there that it was in fact a small miracle that I had made it to where I was at all, as I felt so ill.

He turned up as he eventually had to, walking along the passageway, past the little verandahs of each room, walls painted white, he came and roused me. I was instantly aware of his concern for me, I must have looked rough, grubby feet, having not worn shoes now for ages, grubby clothes, probably an ill, pale complexion, well at least I looked how I felt. I had seen shoes for sale on the outskirts of Mahaballipurham, but they were really expensive for what they were compared to the last ones, twice the price, I refused them. I was so glad to see him, we had both changed noticeably in just ten days, he seemed more mature to me and bigger too. It was a nice protective feeling that he was there to help me to get sorted out.

I drank a salty drink of diarrhoea replenishing salts, lifted the sack into Martin's home and had a shower. There was a spare room a couple of doors down, they were a bit stuffy to cramp two people up in, they were meant for singles and the landlords would have noticed the rules being broken anyway. I decided that yes it was best to be separate and settled everything with the owners easily, before lunch. I did not feel like eating much but Martin was going to a cafe not far away and I tagged on having some of the English menu. It was expensive, but I agreed with Martin that it would be good to taste some home cooking, it was restful to have the reminders of the west available. I could hardly believe that I read apple crumble with custard on the menu, that was a taste of being back home. I did not have it then, but was satisfied with a snack, Martin beside me ate a giant's meal and made me feel a bit ill, he said that he could easily afford it and why not?

The cafe was frequented by many youthful Indian men, also, naturally the place was popular with the travellers in the region. Martin said that he'd made a few friends, he seemed well settled and happy here. Lassi, pancakes, poached eggs, anything non Indian was available here. I was happy to eat little, but forced down food believing that it was good for me. I noticed a guy who looked like a student as he was wearing glasses and seemed refined, less unruly than the other youths. I think he had on a crescent earring, he sat at a table, either reading or rolling a spliff to smoke. I thought about him later he seemed to me to be out of the ordinary, different in some way to the other Indian folk there. I watched him and did not talk to him but hoped that we would.

Having finished eating, I retired to the room and rested myself in the shade wondering what to do about my being ill. Martin had already become frustrated that I did not want aspirin so I took one or two, they helped me to doze. The landlady, seeing that I was in a bad way, later that evening, gave me some tiger balm that she said would get the fire away that was inside of me. By rubbing it on my forehead, the bellyache I complained of would move away and out of me in due course. I thanked her, she lent me a pot of it to continue using.

The loo was visited by me regularly, the liquid pouring out, I drank lots of water, from the tap, if seemed fine to me, chai was a hassle to get, I had to walk all the way to the shop. The salt sachets were to replenish salt that had come out of my system, making the balance of bodily fluid salts too low. They contained basically dried bodily fluids, just add water and ingest when levels are low. They did not taste nice but I did not care, knowing that they were good for me and as I had brought them specifically for this purpose I may as well use them. I had eight, enough for two days if I followed the instructions on the packet, I decided that I would go halves with the recommended amount. I didn't know how long all this was going to last and tummy trouble is common in India so I might need all the help I could get later on. Martin was quick to offer me his sachets too, still concerned.

I sat and lay on the bed inside the room, a small mud floored place with a thatched roof on wooden poles, the thatch being palm leaves or similar. The mud had an insulating quality about it which meant the cool of the ground did not travel easily through to feet standing on it. Although small, the room was cosy, and I had the option of sitting on the small verandah when it pleased me to do so.

I got out the carved wooden face of chaos, this was fine quality carved rosewood, certainly worth a bit, the son of the landlords assured me. He said that if hung near a doorway, the face guarded the owner of the place from bad spirits and gave them good luck. This one was grandiose indeed. I noticed from then on that some other people had them too, many different guises of the chaotic face of the god Kali. The divine protector, the female god of energy, chaotic, powerful, fiery, taker of the souls of the dead in battle, dark and destructive. She is one of the supreme god Shiva's wives, encouraging his destructive side, egging him on, whilst his other partner Parvati, encourages his creative, constructive role. Two sides of the supreme god embodied in his two wives, my current preference for chaos and change embodied in my attraction to Kali.

Chapter 49

In the evening I made an effort to go with Martin and eat. I touched little, having to force myself to accept the strength that was in front of me in the form of food. I met a guy there who had done a lot of travelling and said that he was a brown sugar addict. Without disapproving, I talked with him, learning about jewels that he regularly smuggled through customs, financing his trips out to India where he could get more brown sugar - raw heroin, from the poppy plant, a natural drug.

The habit is incredibly expensive in the west, the man would have had to know dealers high in the chain of supply to secure the same quality of product that he had become used to in India. The price here was of course far lower than in the west, he liked it so much that he travelled often, away from his home, and instead enjoyed the pace of the atmosphere in India with highs at knock down prices.

He mentioned to me that a hit of brown sugar would be healing for me, and invited me round to his place for some. I took some persuading that it was a good idea, so he told me where he lived so that I could come round if and when I felt like it. The next morning I had a drink for breakfast at a nearby cafe down the dusty street. I found him there and said that I wanted to accept his offer and walked with him to his home which he left immediately for, with me in tow. I must have looked really ill as he was offering this expensive medicine for free.

He had a nice big room with some Indian people who knew him, he came back every year to the same place, buying brown sugar, he was a nice chap and we sat down and chatted. He pulled out little packets of gems, tiny rubies, diamonds, emeralds and sapphires. He showed me about ten different types, sparkling riches. I was slightly fascinated by this pirate, taking these things through customs, without a thought for the law, just riding on hope. I thought that this situation I was in was fine, he was not harmful, he was not a major criminal, just unusual. He had recently bought the packet of sugar he opened, this was good stuff, he said. I was relieved when he said that it was, my instincts told me that if the stuff was pure and good then I would come to little harm. He got out his gear, a little browned plastic pipe like a lollipop stick, tin foil and a cigarette lighter. Emptying a small line of the powder onto the foil and running the lighter underneath, he chased the dragon then invited me too. I sucked up some of the smoke through the pipe which I placed into my mouth. The expensive fumes rose up from the vaporising powder. I tried to get as much of it as I could up the pipe as he held the lighter along, otherwise the smoke would be blown away. He said that even having this pipe was a serious crime, let alone the brown sugar in his possession.

The hit felt good. I started rushing away a little but felt very relaxed, a sort of floaty feeling came over me as we continued the conversation and he prepared another line of medicine. The packet cost around twenty Rupees, there were not many lines there. He held the lighter again as I smoothly inhaled along some of the line before it was his turn. A rush in my head then my body ensued. The rush was more of a glow and I began to feel warm inside and as if I was hovering, the conversation was getting too difficult to make the effort to concentrate upon. He said that he did not mind if I left the house and so I did, I thanked him slowly for the medicine and walked smoothly home. I was kind of floating on air all the way back to the room where I lay down, out of the heat. I thought about heroines (the hero's sort) and heroin, as I drifted this way and that before sleep, feeling like doing very little else.

I woke and got some more advice about what I should do, the effect still with me, but gently, not feeling too floaty now. I decided that I was to fast, except for fruit and water, for a number of days until all the foreign life that was in my gut had been flushed out. Getting myself some fresh fruit and my book, I ate sitting in the shade, reading Lolita, about a pretty, innocent young girl and a desperate man who consumed her, then, it turned out, became the consumed one as she, being young, was more easily able to recover from the ordeal. I became immersed in it, spending hours reading, taking the time in breaks to switch my mind onto something else like eating some fruit. Little happened around me as I sat in my own world, most of the people around were out and about by day. I was feeling a little better, and remained determined that I was going to flush my system through.

The next day some noisy German he-men moved in a few doors up, three of them in a room, they were really heavy, listening to rock metal sort of music and smoking chillum after chillum throughout the day. I had wandered off with a few rupees to buy a watermelon, the bananas and little melon of yesterday having been finished. The journey was an effort along the road to a stall where I could buy quite a range of sizes of melon for the same price, I opted for medium, as this was all that I could conceivably consume. Wandering back with the thing on my head seemed a good idea, the balance coming quickly, and more easily, the slower the progress I made. Feeling too weak to carry the thing in all but the most economical way, it worked well. I cut the first slice before reading some more, napping at lunch as the day got hot.

Martin had been out and about, it seemed that had been busy making friends and exploring around the place. I had watched, that morning on the street, a number of stone workers carving stone and finished items for sale, ranging from large ten foot stuff to pocket sized. I imagined that the really big stuff was mostly commissioned only, though one bit was for sale that time, perhaps indicating that someone had had the thing made then cancelled the order. I was gradually becoming aware of a background sound of hundreds of chisels carving stone all around me, all day long, creativity flowed as idols were being shaped.

Chapter 50

Lolita was nearing completion, the book was engrossing so I forgot how I felt, instead immersed in the scenes portrayed. The German neighbours were insistent that they had only been able to obtain shit quality grass and that no one around here had anything decent. They told an Indian who came back to their home how they felt. He would, I hoped, pacify them with good grass before something untoward and embarrassing happened. They smoked their chillums anyway that evening, Martin and I joined them for a little smoke and a chat. They all were fat, German meat eaters I supposed, but they were kind of alright. The hit off of the chillum I had was heavy, in my hungry state the effect was all the stronger. I had another and felt really out of it, the concentration level which had been up for several days was going, I sulked off to bed feeling spaced, but in a nasty way, ready to sleep it off.

Later, I followed Martin to the nearby cafe and ate with him, watched would be more correct, this was as I still did not feel like eating much at all. I saw again the interesting studenty looking type of chap, we chatted a little and he seemed nice, my attraction for him was strong, in a very feminine slightly mystical way, we connected. There were other young men who helped run the cafe, they were young too, they seemed like a bunch of guys who I could get on with. I felt close to them as I did not feel terribly different to them, I perceived them as being just like myself, not feeling the usual distance that I did with many Indian people. There was something really very interesting about the studenty guy, he introduced himself briefly and I liked him. I felt welcome, having broken down the usual barriers existing between customer and caterer.

The next morning I was still into fasting, except for the watermelon, I ate the seeds after the second piece as it was less hassle than sorting them all out. The shits were still there but not as bad, this was a sure sign of my recovery. I sat happily in the shade reading until I had finished the book. I put it away with pride that I had personally managed it so quickly whilst absorbing every single word. At the end of it I had a powerful image in my mind of the character portrayed, of a lost man walking ever further into oblivion possessed by his lustful need for sensual fulfilment.

I had put away my other book, The Tao of Physics, which vaguely linked eastern mysticism with western science. It was hard going, certainly not the sort of thing I wanted to plough through now. I ate a banana, the starch being more filling than the watery melon, I felt that I had eaten a meal, my stomach had shrunk, the shits had stopped by that evening. I now had to eat something substantial as I was weak and needed the energy badly so I went to a different cafe, going round the block from my room. I was instructed by an Indian chap at the cafe to have a lassi and some yogurt with rice. The coolness of the food, he said, would certainly not bring back any of the heat I had in my stomach. They were so kind when I forced myself to eat the rice stuff and found it really difficult. I said that it was impossible and instead drank lassi, feeling a bit better, I then had a little more rice. Embarrassed a bit by the attention and thankful for the care that I had received, the plate was returned to the vendor behind the counter. The

Indian guy who was helping me bought the lassi, I thanked him very much and left after conversation, but did not see him again as I didn't go back there.

The next day I actually managed a breakfast, just a little one, and sat outside afterwards chatting with the Indian lads in reasonable English, about pop music and grass. I chatted to Happy, that's what the slender, tall studenty chap called himself. He did kind of rule the roost in some ways, a presence he had which the others lacked. His English was so fluent that I enjoyed speaking with him more, as there was more that we were able to say to each other. Martin, after helping me out with the breakfast, as I was still weak, went on his way, not staying long to chat to the people there. They were having a little morning rest, chat and puff outside the restaurant and I participated, having a few sucks of beedie. Soon joints started getting passed around, breakfast had finished and the cafe was in the morning lull before lunch. I did not know which of the lads there managed the restaurant, but they did it well, and had a good time too. One of the lads went into the cafe to do some work and the rest of us lazed, smoked and chatted, then the guy that had popped in came out with loads of chai for everyone. This was on the house and I thanked them greatly for their hospitality, they did make me feel honoured. I stayed until half the morning had disappeared, then said goodbye and went off to find Martin, telling them that I'd see them soon, perhaps the next day for breakfast. Martin was not around at the rooms, I was feeling tired and a little stoned so I slept for a bit.

Martin later came back, and we went for lunch, I tried to explain that I was really getting into something here, these people that I was chatting with were real Indians and I was having real conversations with them. It was unsophisticated banter, but I felt I genuinely had something in common with these people from another side of the world, this did excite me and I was glad to have found some friends. They were special to me as the common ground we had covered already surpassed the racial and cultural barriers. Some of the lads were wearing westernised styles of clothing, they all seemed to me to be into the western mentality, with a large dose of Indianism thrown in. Martin warned me later that day that I was chatting and hanging out with dodgy people, he did not think it was right. I suppose I appreciated his caring for me but didn't feel that I wanted or needed to take heed of the warning given, after all I was becoming friends with these people, not just hanging out with them.

He told me about a woman he had met, we went to see her, she was full of life, lots of go, a lively girl, with blonde hair, she was travelling alone. I found her attractive, and thought that there may have been the possibility that there was some chance of romance, wasting time in pleasurable pursuits. We had a common interest in Pentangle, the folk band, and I said that it would be great to play some music together, we were not much on the same wavelength though and it never came off. Martin however became closer and closer friends with her, and must have felt a bit of disappointment when a friend of hers suddenly turned up in the area and they lodged together.

He remained friendly with her and told me of his plans. A few days later he was going off with her and her friend, to visit some of the countryside area in which were exquisite regions and abandoned ancient temples built on hills. The historical importance of these places was significant and they would be gone for several days. That was cool with me, I didn't wish to go so we were again to be parted, until Martin returned.

Chapter 51

Meanwhile I continued pursuing my friendship with the lads as I liked to call them, we had now smoked a little more together outside of the cafe as people walked by, I had also visited the house where Happy lived. It was a simple place but very nice, we went there one evening, listening to great music and smoking beedies. It was a fine thing to have a bit of western music again, the little speakers plugged into the Walkman giving a gentle sound that quickly ran the batteries down. There was an element of mysticism about Happy and that is why I pursued him as he just seemed very interesting to me. He spoke perfect English and had a sort of superiority compared to everyone else with bags of confidence. To me he seemed to have made it in some way, he was quite western in aspects of his outlook, selfish and greedy too, but nevertheless, he rose up out of the chaos which is humanity in India and talked a lot of sense.

The district where he was brought up was Kerela which is the state with the highest level of education in India, he was knowledgeable enough to know better than to toil away endlessly for a pittance of a living. He knew deep down within him that there are other ways to survive, this he was doing, and that attracted me. The salesman qualities that he had about himself, with a reckless regard for having a good time, were qualities that I shared with him, so as mates we got on together, and started to spend quite a bit of time together. I was honoured that he wanted my friendship, and it was a genuinely symbiotic relationship where we helped each other. He was of course poorer than me so I tended to pay for things, he had a detailed local knowledge of the people and places in that overwhelming culture and of the survival instincts needed. He somehow retained more of an individual identity than many people I met there. In this regard he might have had some sort of knowledge that I was interested to know more about, how to retain identity within the midst of the surrounding cultural chaos.

We walked up to the ancient rocks to view the sunset, it was a daily thing that many people did, we sat and smoked on a chillum, passed round in a circle, I had a hit or two, others provided the grass. Relaxing as the sun set, I walked away, long after many others had returned and the sun had all but gone. I was at peace meditating on the glow of the fading sun in the distance with an infinite plain stretching out before me made up of fields worked since ancient times.

A woman walked along one of the connecting paths running between the watery blocks of the paddy fields, behind her were children following, they were on their way back, after a day's work on the fields, walking among the handiwork they might call their own. They fitted into the scene perfectly, no actor being able to capture the harmony they had with their surroundings, this massive artistic creation of patchwork which simultaneously functioned to feed the people. I watched silently and peacefully their walk along the path, the field workers were helping us by growing food, doing the same as had been done for many years, decades, centuries, before that. For me to experience the work that was going on there was like looking back through time into the past, of life long ago. But this was no book that I was reading, the past was happening before my eyes, and there was no chance to close the book and opt out. All around me were farm field workers, toiling away, growing for the population of the town, food that I was eating and that everyone else was eating. I guess the labour was one of love on the part of the farmers as they would be sure to have only a little income from their endeavours, not being able to afford any luxurious lifestyle as a reward for their efforts.

I had come from the future, from London with all the technological devices which are commonly believed to be superior as to make life easier, to take dullness and the humdrum out of ordinary living by letting the machines do the boring work. To witness the toil and ardour of everyday monotonous work was beautiful, like nothing I had seen, there was no question the work was repetitive but there was love in the people doing it. It seemed fitting and right that the work being done was a continuation, there was something reassuring about it all as there was a proven track record of the success of what they were doing. In contrast, western technologies had only been a relatively short time in existence, a great risk was being made, a venturing into the unknown. I already had many negative feelings around these new technologies, I knew that they were not always used well or for their original purposes.

Comforting, was what those farmers were, I thought that I could never be like them and yet I dearly wanted that ancient stabilising experience that they had every day of their lives. The infinite peace they seemed to have as they walked along the paths, knowing that it had been a good day's/ week's/ month's/ lifetime's work and feeling the reassurance of knowing that it was true they had done their best. It was something I had never done, toiled in this type of repetitious farming, I wanted to have it under my belt, to claim it as an experience because it was so different and it did not seem too bad to do. It would not be a permanent thing for me, I could always change whenever I wanted too.

Chapter 52

I sat and thought deeply another evening on the rocks. There were many westerners, excessing on marijuana, lounging around, doing very little and nobody seemed to care that this was the case. It didn't seem to matter to most of the people there that they had travelled all this way to Mahaballipurham to meet with these Indians and to learn from their culture, and also to teach the Indians helpful aspects of their own culture. What was going on was not animated conversation or excitement and anticipation of the possibilities of the cultural crossover, the knowledge that might be gained. Instead, the majority of people were interested in becoming more and more stoned, becoming gradually oblivious of the whole, unique experience that was on offer. Instead, we dulled it all out with the marijuana, shutting down, and just externally ticked over on a minimal survivalist level while we whizzed about in our heads. Not caring about the problems of the world, but dulling out even the love that existed for the world, just sitting there and taking a big break from reality, uncaring about the future of the common good. Instead just caring about the future for ourselves, as long as we had enough money and enough marijuana flowing around our bloodstream then nothing could be better. In this state of false bliss many people seemed to thrive.

I was not having it though, I could not stand for this gross negligence and passing over of responsibility, I was going to take up the gauntlet and change things around me, fulfil the mission that I was here for, find out the real reasons behind why I had come all this way to the other side of the world. Come what may, I was in the right on this one, so, by some sort of divine right, I believed I was safe, all you need is love and that was what I had plenty of. I became heated with a passionate fire inside so I sat more and watched, saying little, glowing inside, the love welling up and bursting from me. It became clear to me what was lacking in this situation, people just needed to love each other a bit more and everything would surely fall into place naturally.

The following days I was still filled with spiritual love, Happy and I spent more time together, we took ourselves off to a secluded part of the dry landscape around the rocks. He wanted to teach me to meditate and I listened to him, wanting to learn. He had flutes, a dark brown coloured one that was his, and a light coloured smaller bamboo one which he presented to me. The bigger the flute, the more proficient the player's ability was to be, therefore I was given a beginner's size of flute, I played and thanked Happy for his gift. He played, and we played a little together, improvising as we went along, me not minding that the harmonics of the result were off sometimes and that the togetherness was not complete. The thrill of making music with this young Indian man was great, I played his flute a bit and we had a joint, peaceful feelings inside.

He helped me to learn how to still my mind and to concentrate on nothing, I said that I could do that, it was easy, so we meditated a bit and I felt stronger afterwards. There was great pleasure in letting so little pass through my mind, I carried on at it, concentrating on stillness, I felt I was getting the hang of it. Soon however I wanted to do something else, as all this school-like concentration was getting me down, other people passed by and joined us, together we had a little smoke before they left again, Happy returned with them while I continued to sit in peace on the rocks as the sun continued to set.

The realisation that all you need is love had a childish simplicity to it, so I set about my work, loving anyone and everyone, with a fervour that felt good, like I was working hard. I was filled with love and was going to give as much as I had away, I knew that it felt good to do so and I knew that I could do it too, so I did, like there was no tomorrow. My flute ability was good enough to get this concept out in the open to the others there, so I played, knowing that I had an audience. A particularly passionate piece turned the head of a westerner further down, over on another part of the rocks, he made a face to say – shut up that's too intense. But I carried on in a lighter vein, a loving one which grew and filled me with love too. It felt like some strange kind of divine blessing was on me that I took in my stride, it certainly energised me and I did not lose the feeling all that evening.

Chapter 53

We went up to the rocks again for a new sunset, meeting there we sat in the peace of the beauty of the landscape around us, away from the cacophony of stone carvers. Collectively we were all enjoying the beautiful scene, immersing ourselves, each one privately in the serenity of the occasion, away from thoughts of rushing around and the other disturbing realities of life's experience. We were here for peace, and I let that loving feeling pierce me to the heart of my soul, my stillness gave me strength, a certain consciousness of myself and of those around me, I felt I was protected and immune.

Feeling safe from the dangers that I knew lurked near, there was the temptation to try some of the more powerful drugs. Brown sugar was taken monthly by Happy and some of his friends, not too often they said, to avoid addiction. I was offered some that evening and refused it, for clear in my mind was that the time I had taken some it had given me a lovely sensation, but that was when I was ill. The reason for taking it had been only to make me better and not to get me high. I did not want to abuse the drug by using it for pleasure, but there was such ease in being drawn to take more of this readily available and stronger poison.

After a heavy grass session I did not mind so much what I took, after all when I was bombed out on the grass my common sense was so dulled that I could hardly figure out what was a good thing and what was a bad thing any more, so my thinking might have become dangerously compromised. It was just as well that the loving feeling I was fortunate enough to experience was cutting right through the stoned feeling I had. I had to concentrate and make an effort to keep this feeling with me, but that I was doing, it was saving me from greater evils, I was being satisfied by the spiritual experience and felt filled to bursting with the pleasure of sharing the experience with the others around me.

Happy asked if I had seen the ancient temple in the area, Tiger Temple, and after finding I had not been we planned to visit. He took me there, to a small temple carved into the rocks with a feeling that it had once been more. We walked around this ancient place and I looked at the doorways, becoming entranced. These large stone rectangles, magical doorways, seemed to open to a new dimension, a thin barrier of writing covered each one from top to bottom. The writing activated the doorways too, I was looking into gateways into another world, with the magical curves of Sanskrit writing from ancient times suspended in the air. The writing shimmered, silver, infused with mystical energy. I joked with Happy that I was just going to walk through one – no! - he was slightly alarmed at my joke. He explained that there was power here and Sanskrit was the first written language of humans. I felt that these carved writings held an ancient secret of inter-dimensional travel to other doorways, in other places, in the world or universe. In this special place, the ancient ones had written their superior knowledge down, unlocking this wisdom for future generations, for those who would listen and learn.

Martin returned, he saw me, I was spending far more time with Happy than when he had left and as he did not think of Happy as at all scrupulous, he warned me to get out of the situation that he believed he could see me falling into. Happy had stolen a cassette tape from him, Martin told me. 'Well why haven't you got it back off of him?' I wondered and it didn't matter that much anyway, property really belonged to everyone, so (communally speaking) wasn't it alright that the tape cassette had changed hands? Martin took the event as a judgement of character against Happy. I didn't care much about that, I was in tune with so much coming from Happy that I felt the knowledge I was rapidly gaining was too good to miss out on, tape thief or not. Martin didn't seem to have made the effort to get the tape returned by demanding that Happy brought it to him. I guess Martin may have thought it stupid to blow up the issue about the tape but I wished that he would stick to his guns and get one over on Happy if that was what was needed.

That was the type of guy that Happy was, slightly intimidating because of his large personality, but I could handle him. He was well known in the place, he lived with Baba, an older guy who was a guardian chap kind of looking after Happy. I felt that the man must have had some good influence over Happy, though he rather liked to drink. I considered that Happy was making the best out of a rough life in India, doing things to get what he wanted meant that he had to be a bit unscrupulous, at times dog eat dog. The western mentality was impossible to run away from, there I was facing it again, learning and building a wealth of experience as I went.

Martin and I had grown further apart, he could not persuade me to change my path. I asked him if he could take my Kali god carving with him and post it home when he sent a parcel, he generously took my heavy treasure from me. We hugged deeply and he parted from Mahaballipurham. We made no arrangement to meet up, this was it, our paths in life had met a fork and we each moved on, we were never close again.

Chapter 54

Some western tourists arrived by boat and stayed a couple of days, I spoke with one of them. Their journey was around the world, visiting many different places on their journey, a big educational trip. The person came across to me as someone who thought they were superior and I felt it my duty to cut them down to size a bit. I asked how they could get a feel of a place if they only stayed there a couple of days and questioned how they could learn about the world by only getting a taste of each place. He kind of agreed with me as did some Indians who were nearby, he probably wished he hadn't met me.

One night I was woken in my bed as I lay on my back by the feeling of a mouse nibbling one of my big toes. It was just having a taste to see if it was worth eating. I knew it meant no harm so I lay there still and silent until the nibbling stopped and I went back to sleep, tucking my toes under the sheet.

My meditation continued, I remember closing my eyes and seeing a wall in front of me, lots of bricks with a thin layer of cement between each one. In my heightened state I could travel right along and through the wall by tuning into the cement that held the impenetrable bricks together. By avoiding these I could traverse the wall and move anywhere in it through the spiritual cement, it glowed with energy, I could travel to any part of the wall very fast through this medium. The bricks took on less significance and this fast network of energy was revealed to me, for me to utilise and use to move around. It was like cycling down the middle of the road in a traffic jam, an easier, faster way. This was an important lesson that I was given through a solitary meditation after smoking, tuning into the ancient powers and secrets in this little changed, ancient part of the world.

The musical connection between Happy and myself grew, I learned to play tunes on Happy's flute, he knew the 'I am sitting in the window ' song from Joe's diner - saying something like he had trapped the soul of the person who wrote it. I knew what he meant, the enthusiasm and skill he had, I understood what he was saying, that he was tuning into the thread of inspiration of the person who had originally played it.

Over the following days in Mahaballipurham the crowd there started to call me Hare (pronounced Hari). Hare Krishna had long hair, played the flute and brought divine love to all people (especially ladies) and was worshipped. This Hare and me were two separate people, I was not being worshipped but instead became in tune with a strong flow of love emanating from me, outwards to all people whom I was with. Indian people in the village that I didn't know were calling me Hare, the feeling was intense and beautiful.

Happy helped me to keep it up for the days following as we visited more places. This love feeling, of being so comfortable with everyone around and spreading love was something that I had been trying hard to achieve and I had finally done it. But what I was feeling was more love than I had ever felt before, the feeling was of being blessed and love circulated throughout me with an abundance to spare, flowing out to the people I was with. I felt like I had an aura around me and I believe others saw that too and were attracted to me as I seemed bursting with it. I chatted peacefully with people and was at my best while I was on the rocks there watching the end of the day, the golden circle lowering behind the paddy plains of the world with the sea to the east. Many of us watched this spectacle, it had become a daily event for me.

One day we were joined by a monkey. I turned and noticed it there, twenty metres away, staring intently at the setting sun, feeling the peace, feeling the love that had no boundaries. With us, that monkey was experiencing the same, how very spiritual was this place.

Happy and I had an outing one day, he hired a moped and drove, I was the passenger. We went to a large hill in the countryside with a huge view and many steps. He wanted to go to the top but I did not so we stopped and played on my pocket magnetic backgammon, sitting on the rocks halfway up the staircase. The game took on a spiritual dimension, an epic battle between east and west, such deep and meaningful truths were played out in this game. Midway strategic defensive positions were used by Happy, while my strategy was aggressive attack, my western ways versus a balance of defence and the possibility of opportunistic attack by Happy, the eastern strategy. Would my luck hold or would wisdom win this game? I narrowly lost, it was a clash of cultures, a summary of global politics and economics in one backgammon game of hallucinogenic intensity.

We came down to the moped again and continued through the countryside visiting a toddy stall, the alcoholic coconut beer was refreshing, it did not take much to feel a bit drunk in the sun. A village man there started to sing, Happy told me it was about his love for his family, pure, from the heart and spontaneous it was. This drink filled man was also filled with love and I had helped him to feel like that, with the love that was emanating from me. Happy said he had not seen such a thing, that it was most unusual and a special event.

Back on the moped as Happy drove, I decided to look backwards. A saying I had heard - that the westerner looks where the train is going and the easterner looks where it has been - was in my head. I sat back to back with Happy, my sandaled feet on the rests, looking at the road open up behind me. People smiled and waved, this seemed an excellent way to travel on a moped because you could see so much, or just close your eyes. I trusted absolutely in Happy to guide us safely, why did I need to look where we were going as well as him? Why did not more people passengers travel like this? Was it because they needed to see where they were going? Before we came to Mahaballipurham Happy stopped and suggested I turn around again, this I did, and closed my eyes for long periods as we travelled along back again.

Chapter 55

I got to know some of Happy's friends. Basheer I met at the cafe who made sandstone chillums, they were a bit wobbly but had a lovely organic aspect about them, being hand crafted. I decided that I would like to buy some, Basheer and a friend would do some commissions for me and they set to making chillums with flowers and vines and leaves around the outsides. I had already bought a smooth, straight one from Boomshanka. This financially-minded business man scoffed at the wobbly organic chillums my friends were making, his enthusiasm for his product, and then my testing it out with him helped to make my decision to purchase his piece, which had a free cleaning/filter cloth thrown in. I had been intrigued that Boomshanka was his given name and did not doubt for a moment that it was, I wondered what parents he might have had to call him that.

I had been getting into the ways of chillum etiquette, passing it always to the right, never using tobacco and cleaning with a long strip of cloth tensioned between toe and left hand, right hand moving the chillum up and down, twisting to clean the inside. When the chillum had been packed, the person to light it lifted it to their forehead with both hands in a prayer position with the chillum between them and said Boomshanka, the sound coming from the belly, a deep, male sound, a prayer and blessing. This is what the others did, this ritual, a holy one with the grass and chillum, so that is what I did. The grass would often have soft flowers and buds and bits of plant all moist and covered with the sticky sweet residue. This sort of grass is rare in the UK, because it is grown outside in the sun and gives a real, ancient high, from plants that have been selected and grown in India for thousands of years by experts. Skunk did not exist in the UK at this time and is inferior to the real thing because it's not grown as nature intended.

The chillum hits were causing visual hallucinations and stimulating my mind into deep thought processes, re-evaluating life as I knew it. It was a peaceful place with the surrounding sounds of hundreds of stone carvers and sunset-slow evenings and next to the sea. My supportive new Indian friends lived in this rhythm and I started to as well. Because the grass was strong and smoked in high quantity, throughout the day, I found I was tripping from morning till night, day after day. New insights and understandings of the world, a fresh look at everything I knew and believed in. This had been my goal, the reason I chose to travel, but I had never planned for it to happen swimming through a lake of altered consciousness. I never felt scared, or out of control or out of my depth but I was travelling in my mind a long way from where I had ever been before.

I experienced an epiphany. I was on the sunset rocks meditating and had a vision of complete darkness, leaving me in obscurity, overwhelmed by the vastness of the void, this scary vision jolted me out and away from the direction I was heading. I took a hold of the lighter aspects and focused on them, struggling gradually to leave that terrifying darkness behind. This was a true opening of my mind, an awareness of the negative powers in the universe. I was sure that I did not like them, once and for all I strove to move away from the oppressive darkness into light. This I had more feeling for and understood better than the formless void, the infinite unknown stretching out in all directions, myself hopelessly lost in the middle. I found that deep down the answer was already there in my consciousness, positivity waiting to be exploited and appreciated, I did not have to endure this dark mystery but could go to a safe, light place instead. I took the option there and then, a survival instinct, leading to a growth of light in my life, leading to great changes, a light- warrior initiation.

That was a finale, the darkness that I saw that time at the rocks near to the sea, mission complete. I had faced into the darkness of an abyss and survived it, with the stillness of mind and loving peace within me there were no boundaries to what I could do.

Chapter 56

On one of my last nights in Mahaballipurham we decided to sleep out under the stars and met up in the evening with a few lads, sleeping on mats together, just outside the village. Happy introduced me to an Indian man who had taken LSD every day for the past 15 years, I wanted to hear some stories. He was not that coherent and briefly told me about meeting an eagle, I think he had personal issues he was escaping from, I thought of him as a bit sad and lost. In the morning we woke and chatted, passing the chillum. Again and again it was packed, passed and smoked, becoming warmer and warmer each time, burning more and more efficiently. I walked/floated to breakfast with the lads and sat quietly feeling beyond high as the conversation went on around me. I had shared five chillums before breakfast and was hallucinating my way through the day with a calm, contented state of mind.

Happy enthusiastically suggested we go on a coach to Bombay, I did not relish the thought of returning there but the adventure had some appeal, Happy asked for some money to buy the luxury coach tickets. I was surprised we were not going on the train but Happy wanted comfort and I found out it was affordable, I liked the idea of a rest from all the busy train experiences for a bit. I still had a couple of hundred pounds with me which was a small fortune. I would leave some things in his house at Mahaballipurham and return soon to pick them up after our trip. My diary, penknife, commissioned chillums, spare clothes, books. I still had about four months left on my visa to run, giving me plenty of time to go off to spend some special time with Happy. A grand feeling I had when I gave Happy the money for the trip that he suggested, I liked the thought of treating him and committing myself to the unknown at the same time, this was going to be taking our friendship to new, previously undiscovered heights.

So why did we go off on a luxury coach journey of hundreds of miles for a few days to Bombay? I guess that it was a change from the scene at Mahaballipurham. It might have been becoming stale with the regular routine of getting chillum- blasted all day and playing around with flutes and meditation. I had been tripping from chillums for nearly a week solidly now. I had become used to rapid change in my environments from travelling about and after two weeks at Mahaballipurham the time had come for a change. I was up for anything with my newfound positive love power flowing out of me to all those around.

I had already gone out of the town a few times, away from the humdrum of the stone carving atmosphere that went on all around. Moments in time being artfully carved and set into stone for a more permanent record of what those moments were, a diary of happenings at the village written in stone statues that I had in some way contributed to. We did not fit into the stone carving scene and try as I might I found it to have its limitations from my perspective, so it was time to do some more travelling, throwing caution to the wind I set off on what was to be my last adventure in India.

Chapter 57

Happy was looking after me during the trip, one lunchtime the coach stopped outside of a restaurant for everyone to have lunch, I ordered and could not eat much at all, I had lost my appetite and the feeling of hunger was replaced by one of fear and anxiety. I froze up and Happy said that I must eat. The plate in front of me with the food on it took on the appearance of the whole world. There was no way that I could conquer the whole world, but Happy was urging me to eat up so I heroically forced down a few more continents and stopped, leaving some food on my plate which I hated to do in India. A primary school song came into my head, "he's got the whole world in his hand" but in my head it was, "he's got the whole world on his plate".

I perceived myself as godly as I was climbing back onto the coach, able to really affect those around me. I would concentrate on the ceiling of the coach and other people's attention became focused there, I could see people looking up, then I would switch to a different place and some heads would turn and follow to the new spot I was concentrating on. I was able to change the places where I was focusing faster than the people there were able to find where the focus had changed to. This did not go on long, but I felt that a psychic connection with others on that coach was actually taking place, the heads were turning, and I was a step ahead of them, leading them.

In the back was a small ghetto blaster that I had paid for, Happy was playing his tapes, to me some of them were taking on astronomic proportions, drawing me into the music so I was only dimly aware of what was happening around me. We had bought a few tapes at the same time as the music box. Happy had bought me some Guns and Roses, I bought myself a Ravi Shankar tape, and recommended something for Happy which was also bought. The radio was not really worth listening to for us, so we just went off into the realms of the imagination and illusion, immersed in the music and its deeper meanings on the back seat with Baba watching by. This older man was quiet, spoke little English and provided some sort of subtle stability to Happy and I on our adventure.

On one meal stop we had the ghetto blaster outside as we sipped our tea and had a snack to eat, the machine was sucking the evil spirits out of the other passengers who were also outside enjoying the break from journeying. We had the machine, Happy and me, we were the guardians of good who were sucking the evil into the machine at a rate of knots, we psychically helped the effect. Happy smiled at me with a look of love that says - isn't it good to be doing this for these people, helping them out of the love in our hearts.

Baba kept on having to be supplied with liberal quantities of alcohol as was his need. I once refused to give over some money when they had nearly run out because Baba was just going to spend it on some very stiff drink and probably have most of the bottle, becoming practically unconscious. He did sometimes share the drink around but he was difficult to communicate with, harder still because I was stoned and he was pissed. I guess I did not mind him coming along as he sometimes had things to say to us, with Happy translating always. I guess he stabilised Happy's extrovert behaviour and enthusiasm, keeping him in his place when needed, providing some grounded wisdom. Actually it was good to have an older, respectable person travelling with us, he kept an eye on both of us, he was disengaged from a lot of what we were getting up to and what we were experiencing psychically and spiritually but also understanding very well what was going on too. The occasional conversation with him helped to clear the air and gave a break from the extreme intensity of the spirituality of what was going on there in the back of the bus. We continued through the night, I assume the drivers changed over as we made our way on, travelling northwest for hundreds of miles.

Chapter 58

We passed through Bangalore briefly and had some time to spare there, I went for a walk towards the park where I had hung out with the friendly students. I saw a couple of them on the other side of the street and smiled and gave a little wave, but I could see their reaction when they saw me. The recognised me but could see I was unkempt, dirty and high, not the same person they spoke with a couple of months earlier. They carried on walking as did I. They were stuck on their narrow path of academia and study, soaking up the knowledge of limitations. I on the other hand was on a journey of the unlimited, unfettered, inspiring, with change creating knowledge and spirituality. We had grown apart so it seemed right that we did not wish to meet each other, I had changed.

It was fun and a bonding experience for both Happy and I, we were already deep friends with a brotherly type of love between us, enhanced by the crazy stoned feeling that never went away. Life is only lived once and so, if you can enjoy it enough, it takes your mind away from those more dreary things that need to be thought about at other times, like poverty.

In Bombay I had a feeling Happy had done this before, he knew the people in the hotel, it was seedy, dodgy and there were too many drugs. I felt a bit uneasy about the wealth I had with me and the fact that I was out of my depth in this scenario. I was liable to be taken advantage of and gave practically all my money to Happy so I did not have to worry about being robbed of my last hundred or so pounds. I had contributed to the wealth of India by giving to someone who was spreading that wealth around. I believed strongly Happy would not do such a thing as take advantage over me although I thought his friends at the hotel might, even with Happy putting them off. We checked into the usual room that Happy stayed in, or so it seemed, and shared a double bed, this was probably cheaper, Baba stayed elsewhere and we did not see much of him. There was not a homosexual relationship between us, just a bond that was often quite overwhelming and emotionally overpowering for me.

Happy insisted that I made more of an effort to look after myself, I was beginning to care less and less about myself, not eating properly, or washing or caring that I looked shabby. In my constantly stoned state I guess that how I looked was just how I felt. Happy insisted that I shower and wash every day, even to the extent that he urged me to use soap. I realised that I had to give into his demands as there was not a valid argument to stand up against them. Of course I enjoyed washing myself and looking after myself, working the soap into my body was a bit like touching something foreign, it was thinner and more wiry, browner and somehow healthier and fitter too. I gradually got used to the way my physique had changed, even washing and brushing my hair, a rare treat that had me feeling vibrant and healthy.

The next morning as Happy roused me he passed me something that smelt unusual as it burnt and said to smoke some of it and to seize the day ahead of us, with this to help us on. He had been out to the dealers on the street to buy this hit of brown sugar which was followed by another small hit, then came the shower. Standing under it, I readjusted to the new consciousness I was experiencing. I had declined at first and then accepted taking these drugs right at the start of the day. The quantity was not enough to become out of control, more just an altering of perception. I felt too the excitement of doing such a crazy thing just as I woke up. I was soon plodding the streets with Happy beside me fending off the vendors and beggars with great success as we went on our way towards breakfast.

The stalls on the side of the street were blatantly and completely ignored by Happy, the vendors accosted me less than usual, he got easily irritated with them for bugging us as we went on our way. This stretch was one that Martin and I had been down and I pointed to the Lonely Planet Indian guide book for sale which Happy recognised to be the same one I had. There were places that were not in the guidebook, so I had realised that it does have its limitations and was not quite as useful as I had hoped it might be. I looked at the book on the stall and felt the authors of the book and the Lonely Planet publishing company were ripping people off because not every bit of India was in it.

We walked on through the town that day and got to the Archway To India with the ornate stone carving and a colonial inscription at the harbour where Martin and I had stood on that first dawn. It blended in with the general hubbub of other buildings today and did not seem too impressive. The vendors were quite aggressive and we left the scene quickly, I pitied the tourists who would not be staying in India for long and knew how their rich appearance would mean that they would be a magnet to that kind of hassle every day of their stay.

Chapter 59

During local bus journeys around Bombay with Happy I could see ghosts sitting on the empty seats, with my heightened senses, now able to tune into what was really around me. Was this a happy way to feel? Just how much did it matter that I often at this time did not feel happy but serious? The grinding poverty, the enormity of human suffering was beginning to get to me now. Seeing the ghosts meant that I believed in their existence. I felt that I ought to be polite to them and became astonished when people would stand, leaving the empty seats in front of me as if they knew the ghosts were there too. Then being relieved when someone plonked themselves down on the seat and cleared the heavy atmosphere of death all around me. The scale of the problem was nearly as large as the population, the life expectancy of most of the people around me was short, they were worn out due to malnourishment, disease and overwork for most of their lives. This is still how the vast majority live. Their ancestors and their children too usually, knowing of nothing different. I felt powerless and lost in the midst of it all but at least Happy seemed to have a survivalist attitude, he was not going to grind himself into the ground by working himself to death.

He and I were, however, still smoking grass quite a bit which gave us spiritual peace from the world around us but I was paying the price of the satisfaction the drugs gave me, the constant intensity of new perceptions wearing me out. I continued to smoke some of the best marijuana in the world, readily available, mostly to dull the grim reality around me. This reality was shockingly displayed in Bombay, triggering my memories and senses again, after I had managed to get away from the horrid suffering.

By English price standards the marijuana might as well have been free, but for the comparative buying power of a rupee it was expensive. The the drug seemed to offer the easiest and cheapest solution for me to contend with witnessing the suffering around me. I thought that perhaps, after spending two and a half months in India, I would now be able to take a philosophical view of the deprivation around me, the beggars and street people everywhere. Instead, old wounds of trauma opened up that had healed slightly in the energy felt at Mahaballipurham and other calmer places. I felt everyone's pain too keenly, empathising with their anguish and hurt. I had not got the strength to last in Bombay, even with the divine guidance that I felt was with me, I was sinking into a pit and it was scaring me that the intensity of the situation was not slackening.

Chapter 60

I thought about phoning my parents, it should not be too hard to do but I quickly forgot about it when I realised that I did not have any idea how to do it as there were no phone boxes and I didn't know the international codes for dialling England. It would have been easy if I could have given the idea some effort, I seemed to lack the energy for even that, and instead my thoughts wandered slightly more to getting out of this place I felt trapped in. These were some tough experiences I was going through and it did not have to go on. There was always that return ticket that I could use to get me back home at any point to Heathrow and that seemingly other world, the one I had been brought up in.

We returned to the hotel again, for another siesta, and I saw through one of the windows into another room, in the same or a nearby hotel. A white skinned woman lay on a bed half asleep, wearing only thick black knickers, she was blonde and I guessed that she was a prostitute. I imagined that she would be earning good money as a white prostitute, though exposing herself to all sorts of diseases, she looked out of it, perhaps she was on some heavy drugs. As she slept I looked more at her, I was not near enough to see her face, I felt she had a family in the western world somewhere. I thought about how she could have ended up in this seedy hotel situation on the other side of the world and that her family would be really worried about her if they knew what she was up to. I concentrated hard with my mind to reach her and to call out to her on a telepathic level that she was stupid and she should get herself out of the situation and get to safety, I felt that I did some good when I saw her stir after my telepathic attempt.

The next day I refused to take any drugs while I was still in bed and urged Happy to try at least half a day without them so we could be fresh, though it was up to him if he took anything. I felt that morning that the previous day's pre-breakfast cocktail was madness and I did not know how I could have done such a thing. I did not dwell on it, we set out again on our day, having looked at the Lonely Planet book for something to do.

Off we went again bravely into the midst of the poverty ridden city, packed with people, activity, bicycles with bells, rickshaws, horses, cars, buses and beggars. We took a bus to some gardens for a break and had some nice things to eat from someone walking around selling, Happy was easygoing about going anywhere, we had a nice free flowing exploration of the busy city.

I said I wanted to go home, to England, the prostitute image had tipped the balance at last. I had made the decision and now stuck to it. It might be a week or so before I got a flight so I needed to go to the airport building and speak with them there. Happy encouraged me to do this so we quickly got into a rickshaw and Happy told the driver where to go. I began having doubts, perhaps we could go and do something else first, maybe I had been a little hasty? "No", Happy said, "we will go and sort out your ticket now". There was a buzz of enormous energy that sped us along through the busy streets, like playing a computer game, the driver careered through the traffic slowing down only if collision was inevitable. I felt privileged to have been transported so quickly and efficiently to outside of the airline office headquarters in Bombay and tipped the rickshaw driver for this speedy ride. I went through the glass doors and past the security, explaining I wanted to book a flight. Happy looked very out of place and did not enter the building, he waited outside, smoking a cigarette.

I spoke with a beautiful Indian woman who spoke perfect English, showing her my ticket, explaining I wanted to use it to get back to Heathrow. No problem, I was very soon booked onto a flight leaving the next day, taking the earliest option rather than waiting for a few days. I thanked her in Hindu, smiled and walked out of the building, with the ticket back to sanity safely in my body belt. What an immense feeling of relief, I had never made such a right decision as that one. Happy was cool about it, I was leaving tomorrow, I said he could keep all the rest of the money I had given him and we would go out somewhere and eat really well as this was my last evening. Again we spent the rest of the day on the streets of Bombay, retiring to the hotel where I got all my stuff packed away into my rucksack in preparation for the following day.

Chapter 61

The darkness of night came and we ventured out into the market areas that were never quiet, blending with the Indians, viewing the stalls, relishing the smells and atmosphere. We got some really great food from a stall on the side of the road and did a lot of walking as we chatted to each other, we would write and I would come and see Happy again, once I had saved some money. It would not take long to earn enough for another trip and then Happy and myself could go off together anywhere, for months if we wanted to. We would go to Menali in the mountains where wise men lived and the world's best quality marijuana plantations were, Happy said it would be great for me to live with and to speak with these men, listening to their wisdom.

Eventually we slept, casually I rose and journeyed to the airport with a sense of deep peace that I had fulfilled everything I had intended to achieve in India and I was going home with a huge accomplishment behind me. I felt that I had learned more in the past two and a half months than I had ever achieved before, in all those years of school. We went in an ambassador taxi, travelling in style. Happy said goodbye to me at the airport, having made sure I was in the right queue and okay. I said I did not expect him to wait for me and we said our goodbyes, he said just before he went that I must not look back, but be like a man and go forward. We hugged long and hard in an emotional goodbye, we parted and I resolutely tried to face forward, but turned to see Happy stride confidently out of the door, out of the airport and away from me.

I turned and joined the queue, there were only a couple of people in front, and I wondered if this ticket I had was really going to take me home. At least if it did not and there was a problem then I could go back to the hotel where Happy was, but it was okay to my surprise and I had only to wait for the plane to leave. I sensed many things on a telepathic level around me. Two elderly people arrived behind me in the queue and were very nice, I talked with them about the white palace in Bombay that had been one of the first places that I had visited. They had been there; they were retired, a couple making a fun journey to India for a holiday, now returning to England. I imagined them to be like my grandparents when they lived in India and did some tourist trips.

These two people were very understanding, I was filled to overflowing with emotion at all this sudden leaving business, and I was hardly expressing any of it. I wanted them to look after something for me, it was the emotion that I felt but could not express at the time. I knew that I was being brave at this time to go back to England and face what was ahead for me and dealing with some of the emotion would just have to wait until it was the right time for me to deal with it.

I asked them to look after this energy or whatever it was, and they understood. It needed to be put in something that had a lid that could shut this energy inside, they kindly found an empty plastic container, opened and closed the lid and then it was alright. I knew it had been the right thing to do, as they said it was safe now, making me feel more relieved. Something they were looking after for me that I could not manage to look after myself. The container went into one of the bags they had.

They said that their weight was too much and some excess would have to be paid on it, so I said they could stick some of their luggage bags with me as I was well under the limit. I carefully lifted their bag with the container in, and my rucksack onto the scales by the side of the desk and off they went on the conveyor belt. I watched carefully at that bit of me going away inside of their bag, it was just too easy. I felt it would be nice to give them a hand in actually loading the luggage onto the plane rather than just sit around without much to do, while other people loaded the luggage onto the plane and sometimes treated it roughly.

I had no hand luggage and sat and stared at the goings on around me as I took in the atmosphere. Then I took a walk all around the airport terminal and used the toilets, this must be why it is so expensive to fly to anywhere, it was so luxurious.

I felt so lost but I knew that soon I would be safe and away from the tormenting poverty all throughout India. I had only seen it all on the television before but seeing it there for real had brought it home, closer to my heart than television could have ever done. To totally get away from it was now impossible, knowing that with one plane flight I could be here again. I now knew that it was real and existed, and had existed for generations, probably thousands of years. I had never before witnessed such suffering and large scale poverty, the existence of it is easy to overlook by simply not believing it. I am sure that everyone who has ever seen and smelt it will always remember. I cannot now forget nor put out of my mind the suffering that is there and I share the knowledge with you, it is there now. By sharing it, the problem is diluted slightly. The solution lies far away, deep within the greedy people in this world, deep within the human nature of people, deep within ourselves. We can all do more to help ease the gruelling oppression that exists in so many places where expectations are so low, where life is so cheap, where so little has changed for so long.

Chapter 62

The quality of the seats was way too expensive in the Indian airport, the wealth that was there compared to the rest of the country was obscene. I think many of the people using them did not see the real India but the polished side only. It is a shame that the standard of the seats could not be lowered to reflect the average standard of health and wealth of human beings in the area.

The Tom and Jerry cartoon on the plane was something I found that there was a deep level to. I had not properly tuned into this aspect before, my brain was working hard, thinking about the deep significance that the cartoon raised for me. On the whole it was enjoyable but also it was a bit too serious. There was a balance to maintain, events and actions in the cartoon pushing the balance this way and that, augmented by the orchestral music. Tom and Jerry were like Yin and Yang, in competition and flux, one being the dominant force, then being overtaken by the other, like the flow of life. The balance was maintained perfectly in the cartoon; it seemed that the exciting orchestral play-out in the final credits was rightly celebrating a work of genius.

During the flight I went for a walk around the plane, going to the loo and smoking a cigarette in the aisle, I chatted with the man whom I had met at the airport with his wife and seemed to straighten out things with him. I did not mention the incident regarding the plastic container. It was nice we managed to meet up, after all there were few people going for a walk at any one time, so perhaps it was lucky to see him again, maybe he even got out of his seat to talk to me. I enjoyed my cigarette, Silk Cut were hugely expensive but in the airport world it made little difference, everything was expensive. I felt I was a smoker, actually needing to get up and really being satisfied by the cigarette, I had become addicted to nicotine.

The cleanliness of the environment which I was now in made me slip back to many of the securities that I realised I was missing. I quickly started to feel comfortable with the luxuries around me, far from being in awe of them all I just got on with it. The security of being back in the sterility of the modern environment was reassuring, just to know that it all still existed and went on was comforting. Surrounded by it again I felt in some way supported by its persistent orderliness.

I felt clean, although not as clean as perhaps some of the passengers might have liked me to be. Cleanliness was a marker of how much I looked after myself. The fact that I had made some effort to keep a respectable physical appearance, in keeping with the dress code of the people who I was travelling with, helped me to fit in. I had on the most westernised clothes I possessed, I felt I was among the rich elite on this plane, the people who had power in this world and I was travelling with them to the land I knew best, England. Many of them were businessmen I guessed, I felt like I was the only backpacker on the whole flight, but I did not feel alone.

I thought that an unknown number were perhaps going on a one-way ticket to England, where hopefully most of the problems facing them in India would be solved within the Asian communities in England. For some of the one-way ticket holders this must have been a scary experience, to leap into the unknown, using everything in the way of financial resources to do it. A huge risk, hopefully they would have the support of relatives wherever they ended up.

Chapter 63

The United Arab Emirates was again the stopover while the plane refuelled, it was an opportunity for everyone to rest and refresh, the size of this plane was larger and so there were more people getting on and off, changing over at this half way place. I felt absolutely confident as I sat in the posh clean lounge, I had my shorts on with my Indian-made shirt, I had left behind the rosewood hand carved pipe that I had been using for smoking as I had been warned that, if caught with it in customs, the officials would not take kindly to the fact that it had been used for smoking an illegal substance. I tried not to let the fact that I was really fond of the pipe matter to me, it had been cheap and whoever it was that I gave the thing to would be proud to have such a high quality and versatile item at their disposal. I had brought one chillum through which had been used a bit and I reckoned that I would be okay with it since I had washed it. It was Boomshanka's, the smooth talking and distinctly westernised salesman of Mahaballipurham - who was probably not named Boomshanka by his parents. My commissioned chillums were at Mahaballipurham along with most of what I had brought to India.

I used this opportunity for exercise and proceeded to walk around the confines of the airport. I found I could buy a large number of things that were of no use to me, and paid lots of money for some food, a Time magazine and a phone card to phone home. I tried but it was engaged each time then I forgot to try phoning any more. I chatted with another traveller in the airport environment but it made me feel more lost as he seemed to know what he was doing, whereas I could hardly believe that I was there and actually going back to England.

I had done so much that it was mind blowing, however I felt brave and confident. I knew that I was going to get back but I could hardly believe it. I did not think much about what would happen when I got home, I just read the magazine and looked around the airport. I thought that if no one was in when I arrived back from Heathrow on the tube then I could easily get let in to a neighbour's house so there was nothing worth worrying about. The chance of the aeroplane crashing existed, and if it did then the possibility of my getting killed was very high, but then I knew there was nothing I could do about that and felt that I was somehow prepared for death. In a state of absolute calm, I sat. Again I attempted to connect telepathically with people around the airport and started feeling apart from the environment there, as I sat alone it got to me a bit.

I wanted to take a walk outside in the lovely sun, however the armed guards around were going to put a stop to that. New arrivals poured through the gates. We had gathered expecting to reboard the plane soon and we all waited in the passageway. There were extremely limited facilities available here and no one knew what was going on or what to do. I chatted with a young man who seemed to be of my ilk and talked about not being allowed outside. He thought it as crap a situation to be in as me and kept himself amused. It was a good feeling we had, of camaraderie between British people in a foreign land, as we all stood in the passageway waiting. The fact that the place was so small meant that we had to chat, it was great hearing English voices around. People were hassling the guards and complaining about the fact that waiting in this corridor was stupid when there were a load of seats around the corner. The seats were for the new arrivals who did not mix with us as we waited, me sitting on the stone floor of the white building. The good old English typically wanting their own way, not easily accepting things as they are but knowing that they can change them.

For a while now, as I had associated with Indians so much, I had observed they commonly held a belief that things would change naturally and what a person could do about it was limited, so greater acceptance of situations seemed to be the norm. I knew that things can change just as quickly as you wish them too, after all was I not suddenly on this flight out to England? That was of my own freewill and choosing. It really was not unreasonable to expect better treatment from the officials, we were not cattle, we were intelligent human beings and demanded respect. There were enough of us to storm the guards, it was just that they carried automatic weapons. The threatening look they had standing there, armed, did nothing to improve what I already thought about the United Arab Emirates.

With a sigh of relief we got back onto the plane, with the passengers having briefly bonded in the airport, the flight felt united, the passengers were happy that once again they were on their way. In the first half of the journey there had been a great feeling of togetherness, we were all doing the same thing, all starting out on this long flight. Excitement and loving vibes were in the air and there was a good feeling around. Now, even after our bonding experience the second half of the flight seemed more reserved. I sensed a little less love, after our rough treatment at the airport where our essential personal freedoms had been denied, this had left me slightly shaken.

Chapter 64

Back on the flight again, I started in some way to readjust myself, mentally and physically, to the change in climate and to the difference in the general spiritual consciousness of people, as the plane made its way from east back to west. There was something that I had found in India and I was not readily going to let go of it, I felt that I had earned it and wanted to hold on to it. But then there was that giving of something away to the couple at the airport in India, I think then that I understood I could give it away and it would come back as and when it was required.

I did not talk to people on this part of the flight much, no one around seemed suitable to strike up a conversation with. A few words were all I could manage, to help to reduce the feeling of fear that slowly overwhelmed me. I sat tense in the seat and could not easily relax, the plastic meal came and went and with it the waste. I saw this as another step towards where I had been born, perhaps someone in India might have been able to earn a living from recycling the plastic lunch trays and associated paraphernalia, this was extraordinary wastage.

Eventually we landed, the aeroplane had been gradually acclimatising us to the ground air temperature so when I stepped out I was not cold, but prepared for England's weather. I sat in the luggage reclaim area and looked around me, I was deeply struck by the number of people rushing around, walking fast, tense, stressed, in a hurry to be somewhere else. I started to feel overwhelmed by these stressful people all around me, it was so unnatural and so unlike any experience I had encountered in the last two and a half months. I could not believe that everyone around thought this was a normal way to be, it was so disharmonious with nature and the deeper peace of the inner self that I had been in touch with. I felt as though I was in an utterly foreign world and that everyone around me was insane, ungrounded and rushing for no good reason other than to avoid listening to their inner selves. I sat and stared at everyone and everything so out of balance, so unlike the peace I had found, both within me and within all the people around me in India. It felt like a strange place.

The customs officials stopped me to check through my bags as I might have appeared likely to be someone smuggling drugs through. They searched through my things and to my disdain found a matchbox in one of the side pockets half stuffed with grass. I said that I had forgotten about that and there was no more with me, I apologised for causing them trouble. They continued to search a little longer then allowed me to repack. Then we went for a further examination, along to a room where I performed a quick strip, thankfully no probing followed. After the ungracious exposure and feeling of vulnerability, I was allowed to sit at a desk and talk with a beautiful customs official. She made sure I got some tea and sorted out the paperwork for me. I got on well with her, being told a few customs stories and a little about what was going on there then.

One chap there had a plaster cast on. It appeared that he often came through and often got stopped (some people do), the officials seemed to know him well and to be on good terms. They debated removing the plaster for examination and replacing it, I don't know what happened but it was nice that my customs officer talked amicably. She said it was good to meet someone intelligent and cooperative like myself behind the scenes as many of the people she had to deal with were awkward, making the day's work a tough one. I had my tea and the paperwork was slowly completed. Then I was allowed to phone my parents for although the formalities had ended I had to pay a fine for the grass found in my luggage, I could not afford it and needed some help.

"Hi Dad, I'm in England, could you come and pick me up, and please bring thirty quid as I have a fine to pay and I've only got twenty." Then Mum came on the phone, she was worried more than surprised, I knew that I would have to cope with her concern when I saw her. I put the phone down knowing they would speed their way to the airport and help me to get out from 'behind the bars' of customs. I decided that Mum sounded seriously worried and that I needed to reassure her, I phoned again and Mum answered, I explained the fine was for a small amount of grass found with me and everything was fine, I was okay and there wasn't anything to worry about. This did the trick, her panic subsided noticeably while I was speaking to her, much to my relief. The phone went down, I thanked the woman for letting me have the free calls and then began to feel emotional that I had achieved an incredible amount in the last eleven weeks, now it was all over, a time to rest. I felt close to tears but did not cry, I started ordering my mind, feeling alone, waiting for my parents to come. I talked a little bit to the new customs person with me in the room, there was not a strong connection between me and this guard.

My parents soon turned up as they lived quite near and thankfully Dad made up the shortfall with the fine. I was free, I got a hug from my mother and returned it. Dad at the time was not so much the hugging sort but I went out feeling supported by both of my loving parents. Collecting my rucksack, I insisted upon carrying it as it was heavy and I was used to it by now.

The questions started later, firstly my mother explained she had been worried about me constantly as there had been no word from me for ten weeks, I had not written. Just one letter composed on the train from Bombay to Bangalore at the start and I had not called. I said that surely they had been in contact with Martin's family, Martin often wrote to them and what he had been doing I had too. Not so much as I thought, they had seen a letter from him but only after they had been so worried as to call his parents. I had a different perspective on England when in India and did not even think or guess that my extreme lack of communication could have been causing concern.

Chapter 65

From Doctor's notes:
On the patient's return, his personality had apparently undergone a total change. Whereas he was previously a very sociable and outgoing person, he had become an introvert, less active, and his thoughts were filled with spiritual and philosophical ideas.

I barely told anyone anything that had happened on my trip, I didn't seem able to talk about it. It was easier to shut out all the memories and experiences until a later date when I could consider it all clearly. It was worse when people asked about it, I barely told any stories or anecdotes about the time I was away. I said that I said I had not written or communicated with anyone in England as my home life had seemed of little importance. Soon, people stopped asking me what I had done because there was nothing to gain, except to make me feel uncomfortable, this was growing increasingly evident to my family and friends.

The day after I was back I visited a close friend's house and sat in the garden with them and their family, they could see I was different, not my usual self. They asked me how much marijuana I had smoked in India, I took a long time to answer this question as accurately as I could, it involved a lot of thinking. I tried to mentally measure the daily quantities in terms of how many matchboxes full of grass I had got through daily at the last stage of my trip, I eventually arrived at the conclusion that it was a lot. I am sure they realised this too.

The people around me wondered and worried what had happened to me, I began to question it myself, how could I have changed so much, it was extraordinary the difference in me. Naturally, they started to invent their own stories of my time away, which of course portrayed far worse and more exciting goings on than what really happened. Because I said a little about this Happy person, my parents thought that I was more or less held hostage by him and suffered at his hands, or that he was part of a cult indoctrinating me. While I suppose Happy did dominate me to an extent through his decision-making, there was no malice to it, we were friends and he was a local and knew what places there were in the vicinity that I might be interested in. The money I gave him was relatively little and I did not believe I had been exploited.

I was coping okay, taking myself off to parks and relaxing, doing very little and becoming pressured by my parents not to stay awake until four o'clock in the morning and walk through the house, not to mope around the place but to make more of an effort to be alive, to do something constructive with my time, like get a job. The money did not matter, it was the act of doing something that was important, being a bit more alive and functional as a human being was required. I preferred the freedom of going to see friends or cycling off somewhere and being on my own, or just sitting, thinking, imagining.

The supportive circle of friends I had were realising that I was not quite right, seeming instead to be on another planet pretty much the whole time. Still they were good enough not to judge but listened and helped, knowing that I had changed because of experiences beyond their knowledge. I started to think that every conversation that I was part of related entirely to me when, in reality, this was seldom the case. During the conversation I would find myself thinking about things related to it, being on a different wavelength, but in some way still making connections between the conversation and myself, for example searching for some sort of answer as to what I should do next, immediately after the conversation, and becoming preoccupied with that, attempting to pick up on clues that I believed to be within the thread of the conversation. So much was going on in my head, my brain was working overtime, yet superficially it seemed that I had shut down.

It became an effort for us all, I found it hard to come out of myself, even moving became too much to handle sometimes, feeling almost paralysed. I was frustrated by the lack of truly understanding people around me who might help me to cope, though at other times I would be fine and able to cope with anything. I felt I was becoming a burden to everyone, but knowing they cared, I persisted in being sociable, agreeing to brief visits seeing people or occasionally accepting a lift from Mum to make life easier. I could not intrude too much into people's lives I could only expect a certain amount of support from those close to me. I needed a lot, in ways they did not seem to be able to provide, I had to find it internally or from another source.

I certainly coped better in India than I did in England, there was more spiritual peace out there, like a holiday, people were more connected with nature. The all powerful loved up feeling for everyone was still with me, but on a deeper level inside, hidden away from everyday encounters. I felt compassionate towards everyone and everything, holding a deep understanding about everyone's psychology and how their experiences had made them what they were.

I had always had a strong empathic streak, an ability to tune into the feelings of those around me. I had never learnt to shut it down properly and so had become overwhelmed by the feelings I had tuned into in India. I had never found myself in an environment where I had needed to switch off my empathy to such an extent, and really struggled when I then had to. I had managed to shut down a number of aspects of my personality, retreating into myself where it was safer. I seemed to be having difficulty in opening up again, the trauma I had felt was keeping me contained, I was not ready to work through it, I lacked the know-how to do so.

I started to grow very sensitive to the environment around me. Having the M4 motorway just a few hundred yards away damaged the air, noise, safety, and limited freedom of movement. I could sense how its proximity caused a deep degree of spiritual unrest, which created stress in all those near it, leading to many illnesses. On England's high speed roads, the awareness of the drivers did not always match the speeds and sophistication of the cars they rushed along with, hastily onto the next place, not enjoying the journey. The traffic may have appeared more chaotic in India, less ordered upon the roads, but the drivers were aware, the chaos was organised in a more natural way, and moved so much slower.

Chapter 66

Returning back to home cooking meant that I ate what I was given, including the meat as well. The food Mum cooked was so rich and nutritious that it was a luxury to have the first return meal, a roast plus vegetables and gravy, with apple crumble with custard. I had really enjoyed my first feast, despite knowing it would have satisfied three people adequately. There was no way I would consider a vegetarian diet while I had access to food of such quality and calibre, rather I would eat too much and have difficulty working off the excess energy. Shamefully, I became quickly used to the luxury of expensive food once more, whenever I wished to eat, there was food in the fridge, I felt guilty with my privilege, having so recently seen so many people undernourished, dying in front of my eyes, I didn't think I deserved it any more that they did. How also did I deserve clean drinking water, a clean bed, a warm safe home, television, a computer, lighting, bath and shower? I had this all to hand but there was nothing better about me than those that had not, I felt filled with responsibility to use the luxuries and the rich life I had to balance global inequalities as it would be utterly selfish not to.

I was looking forward to seeing my girlfriend Reau again, I

rang her house after a few days and we met up some place in town, she wore a long skirt and I had my Indian mirror hat on, still feeling most Indian and slightly alien to being in London. I had a feeling that the mirrors on the hat would help keep my head together and protect me by reflecting back unwanted influences, while at the same time shining out positivity through the bright, circular reflectors. I noticed for the first time how much she swung her hips as she walked, in a way that would probably slow her down. We were at a train station, with a snack shop nearby, we had a little kiss then headed for the shop, later walking out towards the River Thames. Sitting on a wall, looking out, I felt apart from the city rush and talked, saying something significant to her. She had been with a lover and so had I, so that seemed fair to me and from now on mutual faithfulness would be expected. We decided that nothing much had changed between us and planned to meet for longer.

Reau had been a lifelong vegetarian at that point, I admired this about her, that she could be so vigilant about something she believed in so strongly. I chose to adopt a less meat rich lifestyle than that I had before my trip, having now thought about the lives of the animals I was eating and realising they were living and dying for me, just so I could eat them.

We went to an Edvard Munch art exhibition with detailed psychological profiling as to what was happening in the artist's life for each picture. I spent a long time looking at The Scream. Reau and I saw each other a lot, spending many nights together at both our houses, comfortable with each other, just hanging out.

One night at home in Chiswick, awake late into the night, we had a smoke, rather than doze off, we played with Lego, creating a little scene, a pillar with a roof jutting out from all sides, based on a tree shape, a vehicle of my design with additional extras created by Reau. We though it was genius, astounding, I got the camera out, to record this art, I captured Reau concentrating on the work, the speakers too in the room seemed worth a picture at that time. Our piece was displayed on the desk, the lights switched on, some long exposure shots and some with flash.

The epic achievement faded from memory the next morning, although I could still feel some of the genius involved within the creation, it stood out differently to how it did the night before, seeming ordinary. It appeared so different when I was stoned, the whole sensory experience had been altered. I wondered if becoming stoned once again might trigger the same fascination about the Lego sculpture. The most poignant part of the creation was definitely the making of it.

We took a trip to Brighton to visit a friend of hers at a college there. He had an uninspiring flat but was a nice guy, I drove us in Mum's car, this was the furthest we had travelled together and going towards the sea, it felt like quite an adventure. The vast unconquered, undervalued and half forgotten area of Planet Earth, a visit to the big, to something else, to a place that was just a bit different, like India was. I drove us around a bit, the car had a sunroof, Reau got some bubbles, and let the wind blow them from the car while we drove slowly in heavy traffic, bringing joy to all the frustrated drivers. It was sunny, the music was playing, as we left a trail of bubbles behind us. I felt good, satisfied with a resounding feeling of love around, even in the traffic.

We went for a walk in the countryside in the dark and got a bit lost and were helped by some locals with a CB radio who pointed us back in the right direction. When we finally made it to the car I could not find my keys, retracing my steps to where we had sat down and had a joint at the start of the walk. I found them on the ground thankfully.

Chapter 67

Reau's parents were India veterans, having travelled far and wide around the country when they were younger. I'd talk with them a bit, I really listened to them tell me a few of their India stories, beginning to appreciate that there are those that know far more than me, and that I had experienced only the slightest taste of India. There are many who have been there for decades, those who must have huge problems in adjusting to life in their home countries when they return. It would be as if they had to learn everything again about how to live and to get on. Such valuable experiences these travellers have about the other places in this world, such stories of other cultures. These veteran diplomats bring peace into the world, crossing cultural boundaries of religion and politics and nations, uniting peoples by exchanging knowledge. I remember Reau's mum telling me that she was treated as a man when she was there as they could not relate to her as a woman because of her westernised mentality of freedom.

Mahjong was a favourite of Reau's family, I played a game round at her Grandma's house, the long-winded way of setting up the pieces, strict rules were used for a professional touch to the match. Just as well there had been plenty opportunities to get to grips with the game round at Reau's place, playing with her and her mum to learn the basics before this game happened.

I was doing quite well, the concentration was there but somehow Grandma managed to make me slip up in my train of thought, so that from then on, the game went her way, rather sadly for me. She had asked me a question when I was in the middle of concentrating on my next move, it shattered my confidence in the way that I played. Usually I was a dominant and astute player but proceeded to lose from then on that day.

I suppose that I was the only person there who cared so much about winning, to want to win seemed to me to be right, the right attitude to have, it was an incentive for me. Grandma seemed to do better than me while working with different life rules rather than trying to win by domination, hers beat my tried and tested method. Three women and I was the only man, perhaps the women there proved to me that I was getting too big for my boots. I had a problem acknowledging that the three of them did not like that competitive aspect of me, it unnerved me greatly, but I was reassured knowing that there was enough of me that they liked and accepted. Reau and I had been smoking dope earlier that afternoon, it must have been the drug affecting my judgement, slowing my usual tricks down so they did not work so well. I was in a different mental state to that when I usually meet people's parents and so was probably overthinking Grandma's reactions.

I was sure though that the woman had sussed me out in a way that is hard to describe, that led to me feeling mentally defeated. The respect I had for her was great, even though she did make me feel somehow wrong that day, although that was probably why I felt the respect. She was a woman responsible for an entrepreneurial new age family, in that she gave birth to one of Reau's parents, I believed that there was not an ounce of the old colonial style, the dominating, disciplined mentality, in her. Rather I saw a caring, understanding approach which brought change in whoever she was with in all situations, in very much a loving way.

Reau didn't fit in well with my family, they could not relate to her well, I feel she was scapegoated for for encouraging me to smoke more dope. The thing was that we liked a smoke together, so when we were together we often smoked, they thought Reau was encouraging me to smoke more than I might have done without her. Mum believed it was best for me to stop going out with Reau, I trusted mum's judgement more than mine, in my mixed up state. She was trying to care for me, and without Reau in my life, she probably believed I could better help myself and improve my current situation.

A couple of months after my return we went for a walk in the park one evening, Reau was over at my parents' place, sitting on the swing, we talked about people in some country or another who could levitate themselves above the ground. I felt the conversation was missing the point as I had to say to her that it was time for us to split up. 'I want to split up' I said, out of the blue, this took her by surprise and soon she realised that I was serious about it. I said sorry and all those things, I gave her a big farewell hug and comforted her (and myself in the process). It was a dodgy move to make as I did not feel in my heart that what I was doing was right, only doing it as I had been persuaded by my mother. Reau got her stuff and went home on the train that evening, away from me, it was over, my support and friendship with her now gone.

After we split up, I still went out and bought hash and grass, it wasn't hard, there was no single person that I could attribute my continued smoking to, except myself. The shock I had experienced of being witness to large scale poverty contributed greatly to my smoking, trying to escape the feelings and memories. I could have opted for many ways to cope with my problems but I decided to be irresponsible, to get stoned, it seemed easier and somehow clever too.

Chapter 68

I had a problem, I did not know what I wanted to do with all the spare time. I had left school and the permanent holiday had lost its fun, I wanted to do something, but the pressure of a full-time job was beyond me. I went to a friend, Jace, down the road and said I had lots of ideas but no real inspiration of what my next move was going to be. The compounded sum of years of confinement inside a schoolroom meant that I had a lot of catching up to do with my life. Ideas and thoughts were rushing through my head, Jace suggested I get a large sheet of paper and write them all down, he went and got a bit though I was not in the mood there and then.

We chatted some more in the kitchen and I could see he did not understand what was up with me. It was becoming hard to get used to no one around me understanding, feeling like a circus freak might have been only slightly worse an experience. We went to the front garden, it was a sunny day, and talked more, I said it was just the smoking that was doing it even though I did not believe that myself. He said that I could rely on him for help if I needed it. I said little at the time about his offer but I deeply appreciated it. He treated me as a mate, an individual who was in a bit of trouble and might be needing a helping hand, a more down to earth reaction than many people had shown.

I ended up becoming a regular visitor to his garage out the back of his parents' house, chatting with him and his friend who helped there and who nicknamed me Ears. They worked on lots of different cars and

I became involved now and again with car adventures, a notable one was 'borrowing' my Dad's powerful car to tow a trailer to collect a heavy Jaguar car, then nearly rolling the lot when a severe speed wobble built up on the motorway. I told my Dad about it twenty years later.

The brainstorming sheet of paper was used at a later time and all activities that were possible over the next several years went on it, from major projects to minor events. Do an Environmental Science A Level or another A Level, get a part-time job with an agency or otherwise, live in a community, work for Greenpeace, work more with conservation, help the environment, garden work, have a bicycle repair workshop, try care work, undertake other courses, university was also on the cards due to all the qualifications I had. That was one thing I was good at, learning. Perhaps an Environmental Chemistry or Environmental Science degree course, they sounded good. Over the next few years I ended up doing pretty much everything on my list.

Chapter 69

I had so much support, surely all that I needed, but yet what was wrong? No one around me knew what to do or how to relate to me in the world my mind inhabited. Professional help was required, I had retreated away from reality, the real world, into my own safe zone. It was a way to protect myself from the harsh outside world, the one I could not handle, the one I had lost the ability to face. From a flamboyant happy-go-lucky personality, I was becoming depressed and succumbing to it without the knowledge to help myself. After some reluctance I got to know Betty, she gave me her time, talking with me at her at her practice. I did not like seeing a psychiatrist as it signified to me that I was actually ill, but I realised I was desperate enough that I needed to give it a go. I was scared, I did not know what was going on with me, I had shut down my systems to emergency auxiliary power only, recharging and healing internally as much as I could. I was now assisted by pills, prescribed by Betty as a further reminder of my illness.

The secretary Betty employed was the mother of a school friend, she walked with me to her job, from her home, then on the tube, so we saw Betty together, I had the first appointment of the day. Thankfully this made it all seem more of a friendly affair, less daunting and formal. When I met Betty we talked a bit, introducing ourselves and she reflected on people she knew who had travelled. One story about an Indian man who carried around a bag of gemstones that he showed to people, he must have been quite rich to behave this way. I thought Betty was cool, that was essential to my cooperating with her. I felt I wanted to make the extraordinary effort required to bring myself out of myself, once I was doing this I believed I would start to feel better quicker and quicker.

The first session went well, I did not say much but talked a bit about Happy and found out a little about Betty's job situation. She was dedicated, I thought, to what she was doing, to be in smelly London right next to a main road helping out people like me when she could be doing something else. The fact that she enjoyed what she was doing in the session helped relax me, that I was not keeping her from anything she might rather be doing because I was there, taking up her time. I enquired after a few weeks about how much she charged per session, this also became another incentive for me to try hard to get myself straight.

It did work, seeing Betty, but it was just a part of my journey. During the beginning of our sessions together I smoked dope now and again, after smoking the day before the second session I clearly remember that I felt obviously less alert than I had been in the first session, when I felt I had my mental defences in place. It was harder to protect myself from the outside world when I had smoked, during the few days after that session with Betty I let the experiment run the other way. I stopped smoking for a while and liked feeling a bit fresher, coming out of myself a bit more. Until of course I had another smoke and put a pause on the feeling of recovery, the hard work done.

During the third or fourth session Betty convinced me that it was the marijuana that was warping my perception of reality and having a dampening effect on my personality, encouraging the introvert at the expense of the extrovert. I submitted, realising that I was incredibly stupid to have overlooked the most major thing that might have been causing the trouble. Until then, I had thought smoking was actually helping me in some way, but I had become addicted to it instead. Realising in my mind that the smoking was the cause of my current troubles, I decided that when I craved a smoke again I would endure the discomfort of abstaining. The psychological pain of being stoned was, in the long run, far worse than the short term discomfort from an unmet urge to smoke. I stopped, the urge wore down, and I kept taking the pills. I was not entirely sure about them but after some thought became convinced that some part of the vast medical field of knowledge must have been able to come up with something that would do more good than harm.

It seemed to me that Betty was in her seventies, so imagine how brilliant it was that her mum served me tea and biscuits and had a chat while I waited to go in. Because her mum was older, and therefore wiser, I began to think that this short exchange before the session was actually the most important part of the session, and so ate a lot of biscuits and had small chats. With Betty I could talk freely without fear of judgement or ridicule to someone that had more understanding of my perspective than my friends and family. She helped psychologically and the prescribed tablets helped chemically too, a dual approach, with her mum overseeing everything.

The pills were Stelazine, little blue, round, squashed spheres. I decided straight away that they were going to do me some harm but I needed them so much that I decided the possibility of their side effects was worth enduring. The hole that I had chilum blasted in my head now began to close, I could feel it. I was stopping unwelcome thoughts with the help of the Stelazine. A shell was forming around the central part of my brain, protecting the damaged interior, the brain can heal and grow and change, mine was certainly going through great changes, they held a spiritual identity as well as the physical aspect of brain tissue repair.

I met up with a primary school friend whom I had not seen for many years, he was around in the Chiswick area and had got me some hash. It was good to see him but it ended up that we did not see much of each other. Now that I had made this decision about not smoking I decided to tell my mother about the lump of hash. She suggested strongly that I flushed it down the toilet, I agreed. I gradually, slowly, burnt the end with a lighter, crumbled it into the toilet and then burned the end again, and crumbled more into the loo. I flushed the particles away and repeated until I had made myself crumble the entire lump and flush it all away, three flushes. It was gone and could no longer tempt me away from the path I needed to tread.

I received a short and, I thought, partial telegram from Martin which ended something like Happy in India. My mind started making connections between Happy and India and Martin. Had he met Happy? Was Martin continuing with the quest I had left off? No, I forced my mind to stay with the logical interpretation, that my friend was enjoying India and was still there, he was feeling happy, a month after I had returned, and was wishing me well.

Chapter 70

Finding some work was important as I needed my sense of independence, at least getting out of the house would be something major to do every day, and stop me thinking so much. I heard through a friend's dad that there was a painting job in a nearby boatyard, I applied by cycling down there and talking to the boss. I was in, starting the next day I was to go and paint a steel barge that was being made into a house boat, there were already people working on it, they would show me the ropes. Four pounds an hour, an okay wage at that time, and the chance to be doing something that would make me feel useful to the world, exercise, company and the chance to get really dirty and smelly.

Brentford Boatyard was a small scale shipbuilders, mostly welding together steel boats. This particular barge was already made, the entire interior and exterior were being refitted and repainted, a conversion of a dull black steel barge into a beautiful luxury floating house. I was given a quick tour of it, down inside there was a bathroom, lounge, and bedrooms. The hull was being painted with tar that day, so down I went with my work boots on, armed with a roller, I started to roll, conscious that I had to do well on this job in order to keep it, and conscious too that I really wanted to succeed. I found it easy and fun, slapping the paint on, some of it dripped onto the mud, some went onto my work clothes and the hull was soon transformed in colour. The fiddly paintbrush parts were being done first, like the area round near the propeller, then we got the rollers on broom handles out and worked over the majority of one side of the hull.

Ronnie and Paul and Bob made the team a foursome, they were rough sort of East End types, Paul and Bob I found out had been in prison before, I got on with them OK, finding the company interesting and different. They did not seem to mind me coming out with the odd weird comment, in the pub at lunch I listened more than spoke, although gradually speaking more as the days went on. I was enjoying this work, except for a bit near the beginning when I was in the anchor chain compartment painting the inside. This meant a clean up with an incredible industrial hoover, bucket and shovel, then a scratch with a wire brush. The dust was pretty bad, I had to climb out of the little high hole at the top now and again to fill my lungs with fresh air, the silvery aluminium paint layer went on, then the red lead topcoat, the paint actually had lead in it. They were working much faster than me as I was down in that hole where conditions slowed me down, I don't suppose it mattered that I was slow, as the others did not want to go down there to do it. After that part was finished, the majority of the rest was outside work in the sun, sniffing on the fumes of the paint all day long, the need to smoke dope was being fulfilled by the paint making me feel stoned instead.

The men asked me what I was doing there when they found out I had lots of qualifications behind me, I explained that I was taking a year off and had recently come back from India. I believe they may have guessed that all was not right with me anyway due to the offbeat deep philosophical questions I kept coming out with during breaks and pauses, as my thoughts I had when working often merged themselves into a question. I remember asking Paul what he thought the Bible was about, I was told it was fantasy, in a heartbeat he had an answer for me.

I noticed Ronnie threw away some overalls that had become coated in tar and were ruined, he had chucked them down onto the mud from up on the side of the boat. I was distressed about this, there being so much rubbish down there already, putting any more there was out of order. Ronnie didn't seem to care when I told him that I thought he had done something wrong by throwing them down there. Paul said 'Oh well', and did not want to help but Bob could see I was worried. He retrieved them from the mud and disposed of them in one of the bins around in the yard area. When I noticed they had gone, I asked him how he had done it. Turns out he had swung a hook on a rope down to the mud, managing to skilfully hook the overalls onto it to retrieve them from the deep, slimy green algae mud where they had lain, seeping tar into the ecosystem. At least in a bin it would be better for the environment, ending up in a landfill, it was going to cause less damage than putting it where Ronnie had. This was one way of learning wisdom, to mix with those whom I had not mixed with socially before, the world has such varied human inhabitants, each with their own speciality to offer the world, it makes meeting and speaking with people so interesting.

The job went on, the wages came at the end of each week and soon there would be no more work left to do. We breakfasted in the cheap cafe and lunched in the pub, we were quite good about buying each other drinks. After having two pints one day in the pub at lunchtime, I decided that I would not drink any more in the lunch hour in case an accident happened, I felt better for it and worked faster because I was now more alert in the afternoons. The team of the four of us were contracted by the owner of the barge and not the shipyard, so we did not have a set time for lunch, it was nice not to have to hurry back exactly on time, with some days going back a bit earlier and some a bit later, the lunch hour averaged out as just that.

At the yard was the older brother of a friend of mine who had been in the Sea Scouts, he operated the small crane, we chatted a bit, he said I'd changed, and I thought that everyone seemed to be saying that to me. There was not a lot that I could do about it, everyone had to just accept it and get to know me again, still, there was most of the same me there, my character took a bit of getting used to and understanding me took a bit of time. I had my beard, a ponytail and a suntan, alongside the often spaced out look held in my eyes, a sort of hopelessness to my face, and a tendency to stare. It was disturbing to some people who took it the wrong way, feeling unnerved by me, or thinking they may have upset me, when really I was just on a different level.

The men I was working with seemed pretty rough and could possibly be violent, I thought, and so I was even more determined to do a good job and to keep them from being upset, though my current, temporary lack of common sense might mean that I ended up in trouble. The piss was taken out of me a fair bit, comments like 'spaceman' did not help my low self-esteem, but I learned on the barge job to come back with some sort of a comment that negated the last one, so as to not appear to be losing the battle of wits and wills that I was caught up in, standing my ground.

At one point I told Bob what had struck me about him since the first time I met him, that he reminded me very strongly of a parrot in the way his face looked. I told him that to me he looked like one of those colourful parrots, he understood, I guess, what I was saying to him. Another afternoon Bob and I were on a footbridge over the canal and below there were ducks swimming about, nibbling at this and that, feeding. Bob said that they had the right idea, roving around, taking what they wanted from life, free they were, and happy too.

There was another bird there a different day, it was a heron that had come to fish in the polluted stream near to the boatyard where so much rubbish had been thrown into the water and the mud. I thought it did not have any chance of catching anything to eat where it was, and I found myself staring into its eye, as it stood poised. It was doing the same to me and we stayed still, locked on each other for a minute, unblinking. I was seeing into the soul of the heron, I broke off the stare thinking it was getting too intense and a bit ridiculous too, if anyone was to see me doing that, what might they think of me.

Chapter 71

I often thought about the little blue pills I was taking, not a big dose but, nevertheless, a profit driven production of a multinational super rich pharmaceutical company. Was this what I wanted inside of me? Did I trust these pills? What would they do to me and, I mean, really do to me ? Were they in fact designed by the manufacturers to enslave me like a robot to make me work for them, embracing capitalism and forgetting about being caring and loving and human-like? Was I their slave now to make them profit more and control half the western world? I had some in my pocket, and stared at them with distrust, knowing they were the best answer available, however imperfect they were. I thought about throwing them into the river and the effect they would have on the animals there. That was not the answer. I decided instead to stop taking them for a couple of days and see what happened, then I started reducing the dose a bit, by skipping the occasional day. That made me feel I had a better balance of the drug in my system and that I was not as much at the mercy of the medical system. I later returned to the prescribed dose when I felt more trusting in them and their effect.

There was another barge to be done so I stayed, this time being employed by Ronnie, working with Paul too. Again, we were freelance workers taking our own time off and working to our own pattern, though I was to be there only when Ronnie was there to tell me what to do. Firstly on the Saturday, for a higher than usual rate of pay, we painted some big long metal sheets which were in the process of being welded up. Next there was a hold in a boat to do, Ronnie was doing something else, so I went down there with the brush and began to scrub at the rust down there. The room was up in the bows of the ship below the deck, luckily much larger than the last hole I had got into. The morning went and there had not yet been any painting done by myself as I was still scratching, preparing the surface. Ronnie was surprised I had not finished down there as all I needed to do was cover it in aluminium paint. So, fearing I might be displeasing him, I took up the paintbrush and tin of aluminium paint and set to work to paint the whole area, over any remaining rust without clearing it off first. The area became quite smelly as the afternoon progressed, I became stoned again on the fumes of the paint but there was so much more left to do.

Friday came and Ronnie gave me the money for the work done

that week and said I should finish it off later at the weekend as there was another job for us to do the following week. That weekend I got up and went to the yard, it was Sunday and no one was there, I retrieved the materials and got to work down in the steel room, filling it gradually with poisonous, noxious fumes from the paint. It was incredibly demoralising working by myself, not knowing even if I was allowed to be there at all, as the yard was closed. If anything was to go wrong then surely no one would be able to help me out until the next day. I kept on surfacing for a rest and some fresh air, a real bonus was working at my own slow, thorough pace. I carried on painting, at one point I was so down from doing it that I almost committed myself to going home and leaving the job for the next week, but I could not let it get the better of me so I finished the whole area and it looked great. I felt pretty sick, dizzy and weak after all those fumes, but managed to cycle home safely, feeling I had made an achievement, externally with the paint and internally, committing myself to successfully finishing the job off.

There was another barge to be painted, this one was being made up for parties on the Thames, a huge monster it was, a freelance job and Ronnie would be giving me the wages in cash at the end of each week. By now I had got the hang of painting and confidently set to work on it. The end of the week came and Ronnie did not have my wages and said that I'd get them soon, but at the end of the following week, I still only had the promise of wages. Early the next week, we went out one evening and got drunk on Guinness and watched a boxing match round at Ronnie's rented room, just the two of us. Later that week I met Ronnie in the pub in the evening and got some of the money I was owed, I did not stay for a drink with him as I was a bit pissed off. Ronnie said he could not afford the full amount and would give it to me when he had it. I did believe that he was trying to pay me but could not afford it there and then so I carried on working for him, waiting for the large wage packet that was to come after the many days of work. The wages added up to quite a sum, around two hundred and fifty pounds. The job was nearly finished, I did not think that Ronnie could have already been paid in full, probably there was more due to him when the job was finished off, so then he could pay me then.

The last night came, we had to do the deck inside, already we had done a full day's work, but it had to be finished off by the morning. We went to the pub in the evening, Paul and Ronnie drank too much and then planned to go back to work for a bit while I went home for supper. I came back in but Ronnie and Paul had been drinking in the pub all evening, they had also been over to a friend's flat and were in no fit state to work. It was dark as the three of us descended the ladder onto the boat, Paul slipped, smashing the Jack Daniels bottle on the side, we carried on in to finish the job. I argued with them that they were stupid to drink when there was a job to be done and got a bad response so I shut up, then again later, I said that it was their fault this was going to take all night. Paul winded me with his elbow, standing in front of me, making a train noise, jamming his elbow back into my chest. Just enough of a shock to make me really shut up and get on with the work.

A new technique was tried by Paul of pouring out the tin of paint onto the deck then rolling it onto other areas of the deck using the puddle of paint instead of the supply in the tin. This worked out to give a thick coat which was not wanted as there was little paint left. Paul then had a piss on the middle deck, a bit further on from where we were painting, so now we had to roll through his piss. Then Ronnie came back and told us to stop work and come over to his friend's place again for a party. I told them I did not want to go to a party and said I was going home to go to sleep as it was past midnight.

That was the last I saw of Ronnie and Paul, they both got the sack for not finishing the work, the press was round the following morning for an article and found that the barge had been left in a mess, I had been blamed for a fight that had gone on there. Ronnie went away with my wages, after several attempts at finding him at his room and two of his regular pubs, a friend of his told me he was with back his mum up north. I forgot about the money, he must have needed it to have taken it, though if he did not drink so much he would not have.

The boatyard believed me, I said there had been no fight that I knew of, and they gave me a job, painting. That lasted only a couple of days as I did something wrong and had to start the job from scratch. This gave them the impression that I did not know well enough what I was doing so they paid me for what I had done and sacked me. There was an incident that happened at the yard at this time, a pressurised gas bottle used for Oxyacetylene welding was in danger of blowing up, the hose near to the bottle was on fire and nobody was near it. I ran and told someone, then watched from far away as he ran up to the bottle next to the burning hose and turned off the valve, cutting the supply of fuel to the fire, bravely stopping an explosion.

I had mixed with and worked well, with people far outside the middle class social circles I had been brought up in. More social boundaries broken and more wisdom gained, this rich vein of experience was more meaningful than classroom qualifications, more precious to me, as it was something I lacked and continued to pursue with a sense of urgency.

Chapter 72

In my head the world still revolved around me a lot, I sometimes felt I was godly and powerful, somehow everything around me related to me. I would be having a conversation and would still relate it all to what I was thinking about deeply at the time, influencing my most hidden thoughts, as I outwardly appeared distant and unreactive, sometimes sighing deeply. I was becoming used to relating to people around me in this way, integrating it with my everyday life. I would keep getting ideas about what I could do next during conversations, also they would sometimes help to clarify the thoughts resonating through my consciousness, I was on a different level of understanding than others, but still connected. A constant quest for knowledge that I could not switch off, an intense cerebral journey without a destination in sight but a sense of travelling onwards.

I received a letter from Happy.

XXXX means I could not make out the word. Happy used full stops instead of spaces.

Dear.Aaron

First.i.would.like.to.apologise.for.not.sent.you.for.so.long.after.having.journey.Nepal.i.came.back.to.Mahballipurum.and.i.always.think.about.you.How.you.are.And.your.mind.and.your.Body.too.I.really.losed.my.peace.for.last.2.months.Because.of.you.I.mean.I.didn't.get.any.letters.from.

you.so.long.I.thought.if.anything.happens.to.you.or.not..But.one.thing.w
hen.i.got.your.letter.I.really.happy.with.myself.And.I.feel.I.am.talking.w
ith.you.And.I.was.reading.your.letter.For.Five.times.And.I.could'n.belei
ve.it.is.you..Aaron.absloutely.i.got.A.shock.from.your.letter.And.me.and
.Babas.family.we.always.talk.about.you.And.Basha.Hello.aaron.BoomS
hanka.and.Pachhapazam.Everybody.want.you.aaron.you.are.a.such.a.ni
ce.person.For.me.and.I.feel.from.you.Aaron.i.am.goining.to.start.one.s
mall.Resturant.In.Mahaballipurm.In.Baba's.house.Because.The.tourist.s
eason.is.goining.to.start.in.July.And.I.want.make.some.money.before.co
ming.to.England.and.really.i.want.here.you.and.really.I.want.see.you.aar
on.I.feel.you.are.great.friend.In.my.life.You.are.always.welcome.to.My.l
ife.that.mean.with.your.mind.with.your.good.Karma,.Karma's.is.Everyt
hing.in.our.life.Defends.what.we.are.doing.And.what.we.are.thinking.A
nd.aaron.a.XXXXXXX.to.you.do'n.keep.any.bad.mind.with.you.and.do'
n.mix.good.And.bad.together.Some.Time.It.will.makes.you.High.And.i.
think.It.is.not.good.for.your.life.Better.throw.Your.Bad.feeling.from.you
r.mind.And.if.your.doing.something.aaron.you.must.think.at.least.2.time
s.and.you.XXXX.It.must.help.you.aaron.First.you.think.about.your.XX
XXXXX.then.you.carry.the.XXXXXXXX.and.don't.carry.more.than.yo
ur.capacity.It.is.not.good.for.your.mind.and.when.you.comming.back.to.
India.And.I.am.really.waiting.For.you.and.I.want.to.do.something.for.yo
u.and.If.I.can.I.like.to.do.something.together.In.our.life.at.least.show.to.t
he.people.where.is.the.life.where.is.the.faith.and.the.Reality.of.the.life.a
nd.where.is.our.divine.too.and.who.divided.the.divine.and.how.its.split.f
rom.the.Humanbeen.only.If.you.want.to.know.About.all.this.answers.yo
u.must.to.find.yourself.you.go.with.your.own.feet.and.stand.with.your.o
wn.feet.too.It.something.great.In.your.life.and.make.it.strong.yourself.T
here's.a.Funeral.tomorrow.At.St.Patrick's.the.bells.will.ring.so.far.You.

what.must.you.Have.been.Thinking.when.you.Realized.the.time.had.co
me.For.you.I.wish.I.Hadn't.thrown.Away.my.time.on.so.much.Human.a
nd.so.much.Less.divine.the.end.of.the.last.temptation.The.end.of.a.XX
XXX.XXXXX.mystery
Its.a.part.of.my.XXXXXXX

Peace.X.Life
Peace.X.mind
Peace.X.Karma

om.Shanthi-Shanthi-Shanthi

'If one offers me with love and devotion a leaf a flower fruit or water I
will accept it' (Bhagavad Gita 9.26)

      This took me right back into India, I could not handle the
feeling of being back there when I was immersed in such a different life
here, the letter upset me. It reminded me of all that I had been denying,
all that had happened that I had hidden away. The letter acted to bring
things to the surface and I did not feel ready to experience what the
memories were making me feel. I had previously written to Happy, as
some sort of personal therapy and had asked for my diary, I had not
expected a reply.

      I asked my parents to keep the letter for me in a safe place and I
did not read it again for a long time. It reminded me of what I had
almost made myself believe had never happened, but it had. This letter
was the proof, I could not handle it, the India memories were too much

for me to think about just then, I still needed a rest from it all. So I rested. I made out a reply that was well thought out and very understanding, about finding spiritual peace in a foreign land and with the community from that land. I wrote of living in harmony, with no division between the Christian and the Hindu and how Happy and I helped each other along with our spiritual path as brothers.

Through an agency, I did a couple of months full time at B&Q restocking the garden section, my favourite bit was watering the plants at the end of the day, not minding if I finished late, nurturing the hundreds of little lifeforms growing there for people to buy. I worked alongside a great, understanding, agency guy. We had lots of chats and fun, I remember him saying 'you're not paid to think' after my questioning if what we had been asked to do was the most efficient way of doing it. Stacking shelves, carrying compost, unloading lorries, these tasks kept me caught up in the moment, and left my web of thoughts behind.

Inside my head remained a busy place, being physically active was good at calming me down, sometimes I would go for walks in the quiet early hours of the morning, cycling and work too were beneficial. My head would make a lot of connections and work on them hard, when I was with groups of people I would assess the vibe, calculating the yin and yang, being very sensitive to the balance and try to help make adjustments in some mystical way. I was the balancer, the bringer of peace, a young, yet wise mystic.

A few times over this period, my head had the very real feeling of an onion skin layer being removed, like an excess layer being peeled off from the outside of my brain and cast away, losing that which I no longer needed, those superficial elements, leaving a deeper and truer mind behind, a powerful sensation. The layer was gone, not coming back, the change felt irreversible, I did not mind and accepted this as part of the transformative process I was undergoing, trusting that it was for the best.

Chapter 73

I decided to do an A'Level at Kingston College, a two day per week part-time course in Environmental Science. It was a long cycle ride or a quick drive, as the traffic never got busy in the hours I went there. I thought it better to cycle, so making less fumes in London, improving my fitness and health as well. There was a peaceful ride through Richmond Park, where herds of deer still lived, left over from the times when the park was a royal hunting ground. Often on the way back I took more time, perhaps not going all the way back on the road, but instead slowing a bit to travel on the paths and enjoy the scenery more closely from the vantage of my bicycle.

I especially liked seeing the herds of deer, who were a law unto themselves, freely roaming, crossing the road at will, lowered speed limits in the park allowed this. I learned that they were culled, that would be necessary, with no natural predators, careful management of the herd was needed in the small space of the park, compared to the huge areas that are their natural habitat. I only drove if the rain was very bad or if I was running late because I was not organised in time. I found it amazing how much more I enjoyed a leisurely cycle ride, by leaving early, compared with a last minute rush which had been my usual pattern for years and years at school.

The class was made up from a nice mixed bunch of students,

there on the results of the O'Levels they had, I was older than the majority but the difference in ages was slight, the difference in backgrounds was more considerable. The common thread of our studying, learning about some of the ways in which we as humans are affecting the world and some explanations of what nature is doing, is what brought us together. One chap was going to be a teacher, others wanted to continue further with their education, one girl became pregnant during the course, by the end she was really showing, we all tried continually to discourage her from drinking coca cola and smoking cigarettes in the breaks, but it was no good, she only reduced her intake when we were watching.

My extroverted character grew at the college, I was becoming sociable, some of the people there might not have guessed I was taking medication for my mental state, but there was the odd comment and the odd bad day which served to set me apart from the other, more mentally balanced people on the course. I would go around collecting rubbish on the field trips and insist upon vegetarian food. Some of the places we went to scared me and I refused to go to a slag heap which had been re-sculpted into the landscape, believing the slag heap should not have been made in the first place. The superficial landscaping I believed, in no way mitigated the discordance and destruction to nature that had been caused. I waited while the rest of the class took the tour on the field trip, feeling the fear of going there and exposing myself to standing on this wound in the landscape and experiencing the pain of the earth. I believe this protective factor set in sometimes as I needed to be alone and dream a while in my own time, needed to escape reality, not to be faced with the grimness of it.

One bloke there kept on calling me 'spaceman' but I never told him about what was happening to me. I did not tell anyone but got on with my life as best I could, using the generous flexibility of the people I was with and the accommodating college system which meant I could take occasional time off as and when I needed it. Sometimes this time off might be in the middle of a conversation which lacked pressing importance, so I switched off, went into a dream, spaced out to outsiders, but resting to me. The guy who called me spaceman did so in the best of taste, with good humour, perhaps he understood more than I realised, he was the oldest person taking the course, with lots of life experience, we were friendly, going out for a drink once.

There were lectures, scribbling down notes fast, listening to such a wealth of information coming from the teacher that it was an impossible task to write it all down. Filtering the information and thinking about it while I was writing it down was hard enough, but to write the whole lecture required that I wrote at top shorthand speed and that I listened to something different to that which simultaneously I was writing down. Of course this was impossible as I would never think about any of what was being said and would not be stimulated by the lecture. I learned to take notes selectively, the notes becoming smaller over the course, by writing less I could keep up. From eight sides of paper on the first lecture down to one half a side towards the end, condensing the same amount of information, this was an achievement in note taking that I could be proud of and use in the future. We worked without a course textbook because it was a brand new course so the notes were a vital reference.

Chapter 74

I read 'Silent Spring' from the college library, a milestone book about environmental damage, unfortunately it still deals with today's situation, humans' short term destructive use of the environment, using profit as a valid excuse for committing acts of ecoterrorism. I found so many aspects of the war on the environment to be shocking and fascinating. I found I had collected a fair amount of material from many sources and started a filing cabinet, stocking it first with the Greenpeace material I had received over several years membership. Other students on the course were concerned about the environment too, some were members of organisations, this common ground between us gave a strong connection, I took the subject very seriously, rising to the challenge of doing something about it made me feel good.

I made some sort of a a stand for my environmental convictions like being mindful of what I bought and used, thinking about how much energy and resources had gone into manufacturing, driving slowly, cycling and using less electricity and gas. If I had made a stand for everything that was wrong I might have exhausted myself and become increasingly disappointed at my lack of achievement. At least by learning formally about the issues, I was participating in a system to educate people. How I used the knowledge I acquired was entirely up to me, knowledge is a powerful tool, and it was this tool that I chose over radical personal action, in my fragile mental state that approach would have profoundly unsettled me.

At home some nights I would find it difficult to sleep and would be active, I moved into the front room downstairs after disturbing my parents too many times when wandering from my attic room. I started to go for regular night walks and devised a non-violent way to help the environment, letting down the tyres of gas-guzzling vehicles. Using dust caps drilled with holes, a nail and wire I could remove the original dust cap, screw a new one on and let out all the air. It made quite a noise, but in the night no one was around to notice. I soon found that if I let the air out slower by screwing the cap in less, then it was much quieter. I would wander away while the air was released, then return to collect my eco tool.

I chose only the most environmentally damaging cars and let down just one tyre. I thought about the inconvenience I was causing the owner, but felt good that I was not damaging anything, the tyre could simply be reinflated. As I became bolder I would let down a series of tyres at once, casually bending down to screw on my eco tools, then onto the next target, doubling back a bit later to unscrew. I let down about a hundred tyres over a few weeks, then decided to stop, before there were any consequences for me. This was enough of an eco statement to have made in my neighbourhood. I wonder if anyone understood what it was about.

Chapter 75

Towards the end of the one year course we had a debate, the information had been given to us the previous week, and research had since been undertaken. It was a mock debate over the building of a nuclear power station, a hypothetical site was chosen near to the coast in a sparsely populated area in Scotland. There had to be two sides to the debate so we randomly chose who represented which. I ended up as the head of the nuclear industry representative team, debating hotly the case for putting the station there, it was great fun, as it was not really going to happen. Being the industry representative, thinking of the logistics of needing to supply the nation with power and arguing the case was something I had never done before, being always on the anti-nuclear power side of the argument.

I became hotly involved in the debate, the construction contract was to go ahead at the end of it. Complete environmental monitoring would take place and, as a concession, a nature reserve area near to the station was to be created. The debate did not encompass the alternative forms of energy production available, this may definitely have been a better choice, at least over that of the expensive gamble of building a nuclear generating source. I felt worn out afterwards, settling downstairs in the student union room. This was also a place of debate and discussion that I could listen to, gradually calming down from the excitement of my debate before returning homewards.

Through joining the college, I became part of the students' union and the library. A friend I knew previously was often in the union room of the building, Bill, a lovely chap, his presence made me feel more a part of the college, because being there only for two days a week, I tended not to know much about what was going on, lacking a college-related social life. Behind the scenes in the union was interesting, I attended a meeting once purely out of interest about what it entailed, it seemed OK, the informality made it rather appealing and not at all boring as nobody rambled on unstoppably during it. The head of the union, Jack, was a tough guy who made sure things ran smoothly and quickly. I found that he had a passion for fruit machines which he claimed he nearly always won some money from, this must have supplemented his income, or perhaps that was more the impression that he gave. I think his rough and ready approach to his position of power appealed to me, being used to a posh, firm, and conservative approach at school.

Chapter 76

I started typing out this book and a huge wave of pages flooded forth, recalling details, I kept on typing until there was no more left to type. A few months passed and sixty thousand words emerged, it was helpful to unburden myself and it would be many years until I revisited my work.

My mind was always busy, it seemed, thinking up more ideas, escaping still the Indian poverty that had so disturbed me. I was pleased that some of my thoughts were so genius, but people did not seem to appreciate them enough, when I felt I should have been more honoured, I was on a mission of discovery, stretching the boundaries of knowledge, but as the journey was so much in my mind there was little to show for it externally. I wrote some poetry, some art, and played music. Most of the activity in my mind was stored up, unexpressed, building up, weighing me down, the journey was not yet finished, so I continued to move forward with my burden.

I took care and did not give much out, a one way valve, taking others' concern, their love and attention, giving so little back, take care, take care, is what I did, what I needed to nurture my disturbed soul, to help it settle. The days were slowly becoming easier and I was less of an introvert than I had been, but it was a slow, long journey I was on and I had to keep up morale whilst swamped in the spiralling intricacies of my psychotic journey into the truth, or wherever it was taking me.

Chapter 77

I wanted to work to help the environment because I saw this as an urgent thing to do and it made me feel good when I was doing something about it, I found out about the British Trust for Conservation Volunteers and enthusiastically joined in with other eccentric oddballs doing physical work in the outdoors. I sawed down trees to help native species grow in better light, pulled invasive plants from ponds, planted saplings, cleared brambles and burnt them. I helped install a footbridge, working out how to utilise the minibus to tow the heavy one piece iron structure to its place. There was one trip further away for two nights, in the evening on the way there the minibus stopped on the outskirts of London for fish and chips, when we got back in, a man was not there, he did not reappear and did not leave any belongings so off we went, I thought it was clever of him to have got a free lift.

I felt I was doing something of the utmost importance in the world, it was all that I could manage in my fragile state, I enjoyed it, though few seemed to share the sense of urgency and importance of the work that I felt. This pioneering effort we all made was memorably recognised on an occasion by a volunteer, an older Indian man who, after a long, hard days work told us all, well done.

I thought about overpopulation and philosophised that disease and poverty are nature's ways of culling the crowded human areas of the world, but having witnessed something of the suffering that accompanies this in India, I felt sure that it is the responsibility of humans to manage their own population on Earth. Not by war or famine, which have occurred for centuries, but by forward planning and education and freedom of availability of necessary resources, to put an end to the vicious circle of poverty and large families.

I hung out with a young Christian friend of my sister Zoe, she was really nice, and we had fun, just friendship. The first time I was with her at my parents', I could see a white mist all around us, we were immersed in it, I knew only I could see this, I thought of it as us being bathed in some sort of holy Christian blessing, I felt a connection with her on a spiritual plane. I told her about the mist and she took it OK, winning my trust.

Another day we were sitting together inside a hollow tree, after driving to Richmond Park, a little boy was throwing a ball through the entrance to us, she would then throw it out the hole at the top of the tree much to his delight, he got it again and repeated the fun, I was encouraged to take turns throwing the ball too and did so, there was a deep and profound level for me in how I was thinking about this, even as I was doing it and knowing it was just fun. The boy's enjoyment and his parents being OK about letting us strangers interact with him helped reassure me the world was filled with many parts of goodness and joy and that I had the right to enjoy them too, not just to work hard on making the world a better place.

Chapter 78

I received an invitation for a birthday party with food provided, it seemed a great idea to go as there would be a couple of cousins and other people I knew. Sure enough some old faces were there, the evening being particularly sociable, I chatted with people, drank and ate. At the party people were smoking joints, I did not, unusually, partake, to people's surprise. I started feeling slightly cut off from my usual friends as I was mixing with them less, afraid of temptation. I remember thinking that perhaps they were a bit boring because they were smoking joints like they usually did. I went out of my way to introduce myself to some of the square non-partakers. Mixing with the squares was going to be fun, I thought, so I aimed to take the piss as much as possible with them and see how they would react. If they responded well then they would have passed the test I set them and would be allowed my friendship.

I got a drink and chatted with the quietest of wallflowers on the side of the room, laying in hard, taking the piss in an overconfident way, I met Hazel, we soon got to know each other by way of my saying: hello, I'm doing an Environmental Science A Level. She said that she thought at the time that she didn't give a shit. There was something about this shy person that I liked and wanted to find out more about, she was okay for a square and pretty too, as we talked the vibes were good. Hazel had been great friends with my cousin in childhood and knew many of the people there, we got off with each other that evening, and I made her laugh, I felt good about it and we arranged to meet again.

This we did, at Putney swimming pool one evening, I had arrived there first, I thought it might be closed as it seemed shut. I watched her walk towards me as she arrived, she was very pretty and mysterious too, a hug and a kiss. There was a special evening on at the pool, closed to the public so we decided to walk to the jazz pub instead, The Half Moon had an open door into the paying section where the live music was. It was plenty loud enough to hear from in the bar so we had a drink there, saving money. Talking about music and other interests we found we had a lot in common and I found Hazel to be interesting, more interesting by far than my first impression. Afterwards we returned to her parents' house to the downstairs bit where we were alone for some time before I left, happily cycling home, thinking it was good getting into this relationship.

I found her to be incredibly supportive and loved the way she listened to my self-absorbed thoughts, realising that they made sense to her. I was beginning to feel strong desires sometimes to escape from reality and took more marijuana, also I would go wandering off on my own. Walking through the streets around my parents' home in the middle of the night, these times alone were important, calming me down. Meditation became increasingly regular, as did yoga, I felt I needed the discipline while there was so much chaos in my mind.

I needed Hazel, the stability of our relationship grew, I felt that she was wise and understood what I was going through on some level, my thoughts of feeling outcast and sometimes despondent, she somehow understood. She comforted my fears, caring for me by drawing on her own experience, I supported her, encouraging her with what she wanted to do in life and not questioning it, being filled with love for her. In some aspects of life, she was my guide, in others, I was hers. Sometimes I would have divine inspiration when thinking about what was going on in the world around us on a more global scale than Hazel did. She was unfazed, interested and able not to take things too seriously, whereas I was not, but somehow we were good together.

These great truths of mental exploration were nothing new in themselves but to me were a real education, sometimes I would be so wrapped up in them, that what was going on around me was unimportant in comparison. These thoughts were difficult to learn how to control, sometimes I would indulge them for days at a time and have a sad, serious air about me. The grim truths that were playing upon my mind, the endlessness of the stream of thought, the impossibility of ever finding concrete conclusions, the ongoing need to explore everything. These wanderings in my mind sometimes filled me with fear so that I was inactive, paralysed by the enormity of it all, the paradoxes of the thinking increased, though there still seemed to be an overall pattern of Yin Yang nature, balancing everything into unity. This mysterious driving force was determined to put those thoughts in my head and to give me an education like I had never had before, there seemed no end to it.

To think my way out of all of the traps I had ever fallen into in my life, to climb out of the hole I was in. To ally all of my fears and to calm my mind, sometimes filling me with wonder and happiness as I realised things about the world I had never considered before. I could not hope to be taught them, I was going it alone, no guru, no books, no curriculum, no exams, no timetable, the university of life was filling me, leaving me overwhelmed with knowledge. It was just that I had problems with coping with the more immediate things in life, like being present, instead tending to drift off onto a higher plane, as nothing very much around me mattered, nothing so much as that suffering that had so shocked my system in India some nine months ago. Nothing I had ever seen or done seemed as important as that, and there was nothing within the education or experience that I had had in England that taught me about overpopulation, poverty, suffering and similarly huge scale social problems.

My scientific school training had not managed to make me slightly impartial, which might have protected me by approaching the problem logically from the outside. Instead, I had been there in the midst of it, the smells, the sights, a witness to the desperate lives lived. I had become too emotionally involved with the suffering I witnessed, empathising with it, feeling it keenly, wanting to absolve it, becoming overwhelmed by the scale and intensity that was utterly outside of any of my life experience so far. Out in India I had become wrapped up in the problems to the extent that I had become exhausted and disorientated. I revisited these harsh lessons at home now, mentally tackling the problem from a safe distance, not in danger of becoming as involved again, as I was not there any more. Thinking endlessly inspired thoughts about everything in the world I continued onwards on my journey, sometimes dark and difficult but always onwards, mostly alone.

Meeting some people, made me feel like there were comrades all over the place and that I was a part of something big, in that there were others doing similar things to me, I talked with them. I was walking along a route in Chiswick with some friends in the dark one evening after a drink and chatted with a dark skinned older guy passing by, making a connection with him, we nodded and smiled to each other. My friends saw and asked me if I knew him, I replied that he was one of the Brethren (a brotherhood of wise men) as was I, or certainly felt I was, I had never met him before but felt the connection.

On another occasion when walking back home near Ladbroke Grove in no particular hurry I started a conversation with a guy who was a bit down and out, we made a real connection with each other, had a coffee and a great chat and felt a brotherly love. Afterwards I walked along on my own way feeling like there are good people to connect with are everywhere. This was just as well, and an enormous boost to my lonely life as a society misfit.

Chapter 79

From Doctor's notes:

Unfortunately the week before admission to St. Bernards he and his girlfriend were mugged. Following this he became very withdrawn, introverted and barely communicated with anybody. In addition, he appeared to be depressed and his appetite and concentration deteriorated, however sleep was good. Over the next few days, he became increasingly agitated, causing his parents to become worried enough to seek urgent psychiatric assessment for him.

I decided to cycle straight on, down the alleyway, the quickest route. I could see a group of about six youths, young men that we would pass close by if I went that way, I could have gone left or right instead. Somewhere in me an alarm bell rang which I ignored, accepting the fate that lay ahead, not wanting to resist. As we passed they stopped me, with Hazel sitting on the handlebars facing forward, they pushed me into the wire mesh fence while I still sat on my bike. They asked for cigarettes, Hazel had some, they took some, then the packet. One was near me, I stared at him, 'stop looking at me', a punch to my mouth, one front tooth forever slightly out of line, we got back on the bike and continued on our way. 'That wasn't too bad' I said, then became aware that they had decided to run after us. I couldn't outrun them with Hazel on the handlebars so I stopped and got off. I felt protective of her but it was just me they were interested in, the packet of cigarettes and a punch to the mouth had not satisfied their need. Maybe my staring face unnerved them, and they took a dislike to me. They came at me, I was ready and held my arms over my head as I was punched and kicked. I curled up in a ball on the ground, arms over my head, still they kicked. A woman who was near ran to my aid, she screamed at them to stop and dragged them off, perhaps she knew them and they respected her.

The beating stopped, I was bruised but not hurt, I was numb, I was silent, something had broken. I carried on home with Hazel, silent, in shock, we lay on my bed together, she soothed me, I tried to cry, feeling it but not managing to express it. I could not understand why they had done what they had done, the disaffection they must have felt about life seemed huge, to take out their anger on a random innocent.

Hazel hugged me for a long time on the bed, nursing my newly fractured soul and spirit, allowing me to feel my shock until I said I was okay and encouraged her to go. Something broke apart in me that day that had previously been very slowly healing, the psychic wound inflicted by witnessing the terrible deprivation and poverty in India had been torn wide open. Those issues were here too, that had been most clearly communicated to me, help was needed by the poor in this society too, urgently.

Western society, with its housing estates, was fermenting and developing these boys, nurturing their disaffection, creating youths who were ignored, forgotten, unimportant, useless, insignificant, no use to anyone, angry and full of hate towards all of society. Somehow India kept things in a much better balance despite the inequalities being worse and life brutal, maybe religion helped to glue everyone together. There was less anger, more passivity, a numb acceptance of the way things are, have been, and will be. The lucky few strive, climb carefully and determinedly out their lives and into a better one, but these youths seemed determined to stay where they were.

I had seen the tall woman walking ahead down the alleyway, she had run to my aid, she understood that nothing was to be gained by this attack. She was angry, shouting, pulling, caring, saving me from worse brutality, she was also brave, determined, kind, caring and peaceful. She was trying to stop these young men further damaging their own Karma, stop them being angry, make them choose differently. She was making them confront their actions, what were they to gain from kicking another young man who was curled up in a ball on the ground, were they brave men, did they see themselves getting ahead in the world acting this way? Hazel explained to me how hard this woman had worked to help me, how determined and passionate she was, dragging them off, she could have turned her head and ignored the situation but she ran and helped. She taught those youths some sense that day, I taught them something too, by not resisting them once, just accepting my fate.

I think that these youths attacked me because they were angry men, growing up in the relatively deprived estate near to the alleyway. They took their anger out on me because I was rich and privileged, had a beautiful girlfriend and an arrogance when I stared at one of them. I did not take it personally, I felt sorry for them, the structure of society had dealt them a difficult start in life, and me an easier one. They just wanted to communicate to me what life feels like on their level, make me understand their difficulties and hardships. I understood very clearly why they were angry, jealous and I would have perhaps felt the same way in their position. I saw one of them crossing the High Street some months later, the anger he had inside was visible in his body language as he walked along. He didn't notice me and probably didn't remember me as he was so caught up in his own troubles, I didn't feel afraid when I saw him.

Chapter 80

I had an exam the next day – I sat and wrote a very deep and meaningful paragraph then sat quietly for the rest of the exam time. My answer focused on how we need to respect the world as a living thing, to respect the environment and live in harmony with it for then we will be looked after and nurtured by the world and environmental problems will cease to exist. I then applied this theory briefly to the question posed.

I shut down over a few days and internalised everything that was building up, all my feelings, I was in shock. I had gone over the edge, past the line between where you are able to cope with life and where you are not able to cope. I had reached a point that was beyond the limits of help from my parents and friends. My parents realised this and took me by car to hospital to get some treatment. I remember being in the back seizing handfuls of my hair and pulling at it hard, literally 'tearing my hair out'. After briefly being shown to a room in the general hospital where my Dad talked to the doctor about a chemical imbalance in my brain, we left and went onwards.

I was delivered to a psychiatric hospital and admitted there, I understood this as another part of my journey, and one that I would take without my parents or friends. I was out of reach to them, had moved to an area of spiritual and mental consciousness that was outside their experience, treading paths they did not know. So much had happened to me recently that becoming a psychiatric patient did not really seem like a big deal, an adventure maybe, bit scary, but I felt that I would be able to handle it. I ended up staying at Saint Bernard's psychiatric hospital for a period of just one month. It was a brief and unforgettable experience.

I tried very hard at making myself better in that place, as there were those, as there always are in those places, who had lived there for years and years and years, and were probably going to die there. You would not find me ending up like that, no way. 'Oh well,' I thought, walking into the loony bin, 'this is it, this is really the last stop on the road towards the unconquerable, if I don't get myself out of this one then I've got real problems'. As some of the longer stay patients were visibly much worse off than me I instantly felt better. As though they were the mad ones and I was a kind of visitor, a sort of staff in disguise as a patient. Initially I was heavily medicated and kept under close surveillance, the dosage was reduced over the following days so that it was maintained at the right level for me.

My Walkman was stolen from a bag that I had put under my seat fifteen minutes after I arrived when I went to the loo. I looked at the others in the lounge and then decided to do nothing as it was insignificant compared with what was happening to me. I did not want the extra hassle and did not want to lose face among my new peers by running to the staff as soon as anything untoward happened and getting other patients into trouble.

Hazel and my mother visited on the second day, after I had begun to adjust to the change in lifestyle, Hazel said later it was obvious that I had been given a lot of drugs initially. A useful way to tell the staff apart from the patients, which could be difficult, is that the staff are the ones who dole out the drugs and who don't let you out of the building. After a few days a staff member accompanied me and an elderly woman called Barbara for a walk, we made our way slowly, so as to let Barbara keep up with us, the male nurse led us towards the canal, a small oasis of peace by the still water. I spotted a barge for sale and made a mental note of the number, I said I was thinking of buying one, renovating it and living aboard, with Hazel perhaps, and travelling around the UK on it, as it was possible to do quite cheaply. My mum told me the nurse later decided to become a priest and I believed I had helped influence his decision, simply by being with him on that walk, in my spiritually attuned state.

People needing intense help and support, the mad ones, are often shut away in institutions where they are easy for society to forget about or ignore. I wrote off people in psychiatric hospitals for years beforehand, imagining them as all being violent, drooling at the mouth and incomprehensible. In fact there was a gentle suffering there, people accepting their burdens and making the best of it by getting on with life as well as they could. The way the place was run respected that people there were extra sensitive to pressure and disturbance, so they were not given any. This gentle caring atmosphere led to a quicker recovery, we all worked at keeping a lid on things and at being calm and respecting each other. All of us patients were there for a rest from the outside world, a holiday from having to worry about any of the daily things we usually worried about. I had everything taken care of, meals, waking up time and going to bed time, a large spread of individuals for company, nothing to worry about but getting better and getting out of the place.

Barbara could have been the oldest of the patients, and I had a suspicion that she had planned our walk outside to the canal. I doubt if she often got out of the hospital, she seemed so involved with the internal happenings of the community. Because of her age, I had an instinctive feeling that she knew what was going on, as though in reality she was secretly running the hospital. However, due to her illness, and mine, it was difficult to properly interpret exactly how she fitted in to the scheme of things. Patient Joe was an old guy there and I thought that together they made a mystical couple who were pretty much in charge of everything, although none of the staff knew that. They were the wise ones who had actually chosen to stay at the hospital and help all the patients that came and went over the years. What an incredible pair of people to dedicate their lives to human service in this way, it was an honour to be in their presence.

One day they were both in the lounge and giving out incredible healing vibes to all the patients. A guy who had been back home for the day and had smoked dope with his mates had come back to the hospital a bit disturbed. As he sat there Barbara said 'here it comes' and the guy let out a loud shout of anguish and pain and frustration about how he was feeling. Because she had warned us about this shout it was totally okay and we understood that the guy was only expressing how he felt at the time, no one was particularly upset by it.

I went outside to the garden for a cigarette with Joe and a staff member, it was sunny and peaceful. There was a sense of how time had become endless for Joe, he never had anything that he needed to do, except be looked after, he was totally institutionalised, not capable of being independent. He had another cigarette and I watched him in his wheelchair and thought about what sort of life he had and how difficult it must be, but also appreciated how he was an equal member of the human race. Despite his external appearance, age and physical weakness, he had a mystical edge to him, indicating that actually he knew a lot more about what was going on and had much more power than it seemed. I felt I had opened a window into his unique and unusual world, how his purpose in life was involved with helping to heal those at the hospital and sustaining a mystical balance of energy.

Chapter 81

There were others there going through recovery from marijuana psychosis, my diagnosis, they were experiencing similar symptoms to myself. The reasons behind each of our conditions varied greatly, each person having an individual story behind why they needed to escape reality with drugs and took it too far. Some, like me may have had some sort of traumatic event that brought things out, I did not talk with other patients about their journey, focusing instead with the here and now.

There are a lot of people who are affected adversely by marijuana, individual sensitivity and metabolism varies greatly so it is difficult to predict how a person will react to it. Only the smoker can gauge their own sensitivity and then adjust their dosage accordingly to their desires, aiming for a happy balance between cost, straightness, stonedness and psychosis.

'Help!' I heard a man call in the dark in the ward one night. I listened, awake, the request was coming from over the other side of the ward. I left my bed and headed over towards the noise. I came to old Joe's bed and went up to him, he looked at me and widened his legs apart under the duvet – like he was offering himself to me. I thought about how long this guy had been in psychiatric institutions, how vulnerable he was and how many times he may have been raped by people over the years, just passively giving into another abuse.

I gave him some sort of reassurance and moved to the bed next to his where the call came again. 'Pass me the bottle' asked a desperate alcoholic. I found a pee bottle near and helped him put his penis in it while he emptied out some of the awful impurities that were in his body. 'Thanks'. Putting the bottle down by the bed I headed back to my own and went back to sleep, in this place where only curtains separated us. The next day the guy thanked me for helping out, embarrassed. No trouble really, I thought that he was a sad case who had so damaged his body with alcohol that he could not function enough to even get out of bed when he needed to. I considered dope smoking to be somewhat higher on the scale of social acceptability than alcoholism - his body was wrecked. He seemed like quite an average guy, not what I imagined an alcoholic to be like. However, several days later he seemed fine and I was still making a slow recovery compared to him.

A square female staff member talked with one of her colleagues about having played tennis recently, it made me think what a different wavelength she functioned on and how she had no idea of how to relate to us. She was quite highly strung and lacked any soft, nurturing, motherly love. I decided to test her out. I started undressing, unclipping my dungarees and sliding them down in the lounge area. She quickly reacted and came over to me, 'oh no, you don't start doing that behaviour'. I sat back down, having now sussed her out as anxious and not very good at being able to cope with much out of the ordinary. If only she would be open to how much there was here for her to learn from the patients.

Mainstream society was far away from the hospital, this little group of us being looked after, treated as special, because we were special. We were elite change makers working on high spiritual levels, subtly tweaking the balance to help the world back on track. I believed we were brought together to conquer something on a spiritual level that society could not beat at that time, it needed the strength of a special group. I was one selected to be a part of this, that is why I had been beaten up, so I could be here and help out. Our spiritual quest, our mission at that time was to heal society from our safe space at the hospital, by conquering something negative and pervasive, it was a focus for all of us. It more than balanced out all the time given by staff, the food, heating and other resources we were receiving from society. This was because the changes we were working on were deep and far reaching, affecting many thousands.

The work that I did there during my stay, I did intuitively and conscientiously, somehow fitting pieces into place, helping bring healing positivity into the world. I had already done much of this, usually unobserved and unacknowledged. I had been drafted in to this team of patients by a higher power so that my skills and experience would be added to those already there to overcome a certain negative force. I was honoured to be a part of this community of elite change makers brought together for that short time, working as best we could to complete our quest, bringing gradual transformation to the society that had excluded us.

Chapter 82

As the weeks progressed I was allowed to take short walks alone around the hospital grounds outside, it was so sunny that I was glad to get out into it. The song by Madness 'Summer in London' went through my head, I had spent very few full summers in London, usually the school holidays had taken me away into the countryside visiting Granny and friends of my parents.

There was a game of football outside one day with a bunch of lads that were patients, it was fun and normal, all of us from different backgrounds getting together to have a game. I felt I had changed, in that for the first time I felt completely comfortable and at ease with these lads and treated as an equal. There was a funny episode when the ball got stuck on a low roof and a guy climbed up a drainpipe to free it, which he did and ripped his shorts, he didn't care and carried on playing. We all went back inside afterwards a lot more cheered up than before, the physical exercise and fun had done us a whole world of good.

A Lord of the Rings puzzle was dropped off by my family to help occupy my mind. I did most of it but it was hard to concentrate. After I had been a patient for three weeks the old ward suddenly closed and we all moved to brand new single, en suite rooms, absolute luxury compared with the old ward of twelve, with curtains for privacy. Here I started a small tapestry of a robin and did some advanced maths exercises from a book I requested, the world of maths seemed a safe, predictable place to visit. The new ward was close to the old one and nearby a busy general hospital, I went into the foyer for a visit one day and fell asleep on some chairs, lying along them near the entrance as many people came and went around me. I continued to have visitors, some friends and family which I found both supportive and grounding, to know that my old life still existed to go back to.

I was smoking cigarettes and remember being encouraged by staff to slow down and enjoy them, 'don't smoke them too fast because they don't burn properly', good advice. I bought some from a shop over the road and also asked if they sold them one at a time, as this used to be practice in some shops. They gave me a small bag filled with all sorts of single cigarettes of different brands, about fifty in all. I carried this back towards the hospital but then felt that I did not want it as it was not mine, it belonged to lots of other people who had bought single cigarettes and been ripped off by the inflated price. I put the bag in a bin, wandered along and thought for a while about this decision, sitting quietly in the sunshine near the busy street. I changed my mind, thinking that I could give them to patients, I walked back to the bin to take them again. They were gone, someone with sharp eyes and a need for cigarettes had spotted the prize I had left, it was good they went to someone who needed them.

I thought the grounds surrounding the hospital were messy, there was rubbish there which I cleared up and put into bins. Also there were huge areas of weeds which I took it upon myself to clear out from some of the flower beds. I swished at them with a stick sending the dandelion seeds floating about everywhere, levelling the weed jungle. It was great fun and rewarding to think that I was making myself useful. I was also acting on a recurring thought of 'do eye' that regularly came to me, I was doing something about how things looked and getting pretty much an instant result from my actions - doing eye. Part of my purpose of being at the hospital, to make the environment better. At one point I decided to iron my pyjamas and other clothes from the laundry, 'you are a good boy' said the kind Indian woman who worked there.

On one occasion in the hospital I spent time with a smiley lad of about twenty who was of Indian origin, I chatted with him and he agreed to have a game of chess with me. We sat down together, I set up the board and play commenced. I moved a pawn and he moved whatever piece took his fancy, wherever he wished. I could tell from the drugged state of this guy and his expression that he believed his moves were okay. I had a think and worked out a strategy for the game - I was going to play by the rules I knew and let him do things his way. After playing for a while I realised I was going to be annihilated and so, as the end of the game was coming, I adopted a looser interpretation of the rules and matched his anarchic style in deciding which pieces I was going to take and then moving a random piece to take it - I enjoyed taking his powerful pieces with my pawns. He seemed glad that I had adjusted to his style of play and the game soon ended. I tried to chat a bit but his English was limited, yet I was satisfied with this level of connection and friendship that I had achieved with an English Indian, with smiles and a chess game.

I enjoyed one session of art therapy, which was held in another part of the hospital, a magical, beautiful young couple gave me paper and paints, we sat at tables in a big art room. They showered each of us patients with love, good vibes and permission for creative freedom, validating everyone's work, however humble their creation. I had so much to express and became completely focused on my picture in which I attempted to portray all the truths about all the connections between everything that was on my mind. Different symbolic images connected with each other, it was a huge and profound expression of my state of mind and the complex web of interconnectivity, I tried to represent themes of nature and its laws, overlaid with the unnatural laws of humans which work against the innate order of the world. I have it still, framed on my wall. I only went to one art therapy session as I was not a patient long, I found it to be such a freeing experience, I gained so much from it, a pressure valve had been released by this depth of self expression.

In the hospital there was a time where I felt that I was battling with negative spirits that were around in the old sections of the hospital that had closed down. This was an important contribution to the overall mission that all us patients were on, and helped to keep the spiritual environment around us safe. I felt I was being guided towards negativity that I could overcome and away from that which I could not, quickly learning more skills and turning more things around from negative to positive, with a sense of urgency and purpose. There were times when I felt surrounded by spiritual toxicity. In response I used an imaginary, fully effective, gas mask that I just pulled down to cover over my nose and mouth, then carried on with my mission.

During this period I had a constant awareness of spiritual happenings around me, I felt there to be spirits present, both powerful ones that induced good vibes and feelings of euphoria, and others that were darker and sadder, sometimes even malevolent. Intuitively I avoided those that felt negative. I used my natural, caring nature in these circumstances and tried to balance being open and receptive towards the spirits with protecting myself from those that were dangerous and might play deceitful games on vulnerable people. This awareness of spirits was similar to seeing the spirits on the bus at the end of my stay in India, I was tuning into another aspect of reality as part of my general increase in spiritual knowledge and perception over this period. This sense was now awakened in me and I had some basic training in it too, guided by wise ones in the hospital. I was able to tune in and tune out safely of the spirit world and continued to have an awareness for many years afterwards as I got on with my life.

Chapter 83

From Doctor's notes:

Initially he remained withdrawn and appeared generally suspicious about his environment. However, he did not exhibit any overt hallucinations but initially remained somewhat thought disordered. Gradually, his mental state improved and he became less suspicious, more conversant and sociable, revealing a sensitive and interesting young man who was able to mix easily with the members of the ward staff and the other patients.

I later got onto the occupational therapy part of the recovery process, towards the end they encouraged me to do things, within the hospital grounds, car valeting or gardening. Gardening out in the sun was great, watering the plants, tying tomato plants to sticks with soft bits of tights so as not to damage the stalk. Danny, the gardener there, was a very nice lad, a friendly bloke. He had a cigarette lighter that could have been used for welding, the flame made a roaring sound as it burned with a blue cone, this neat little gadget was a bit overpowered as a cigarette lighter but it did the trick. I liked the gardening, enjoying being with nature and helping the plants, eating tomatoes, chatting with other patients and drinking tea, Danny took to me and I took to him.

After discharge my recovery programme gradually wound down and my connection with Saint Bernard's loosened, I would visit once a week for therapeutic gardening sessions with the doctors there seeing me now and again, checking my progress. I'd cycle there or more often drive in Mum's car and hang out, gently working in the garden with Danny and patients. On one visit as I waited to see the psychiatrist he was chatting with his colleague in the adjoining office and I watched them. They were joking and having fun and I became convinced they were talking about a rave that they had been to at the weekend and that they had both taken Ecstasy and danced the night away. I felt good about the idea that they had a human, down to earth side to their personalities but felt less trusting towards their capacity to do a good job in their highly responsible positions.

It was at my last session that Danny showed me a high staircase where a patient had thrown themselves down, ending up permanently in a wheelchair due to the injuries they sustained. He said the patient had been a lovely young man just like me and that I reminded him a lot of that person. We went for lunch with Danny's Indian girlfriend, she was very much a Londoner, it was nice to hear her speak with an English accent, she worked in the hospital too as an administrator, they lived together in one of the staff homes on site. I enjoyed his informality and how he just wanted to help people, and how his girlfriend was totally okay about me joining them while they both had their lunch break.

Some yoga for people with mental health issues was offered in Chiswick as another part of my recovery process. I went to a few of these sessions which were run by an Indian woman, she often had us curl up in a ball and rock ourselves on our back, a bit like a mother soothing her distressed babies, it helped. By this point I had been back home for fifteen months.

Chapter 84

I hung out a bit with Jamie who I had known at primary school, he lived in Chiswick and because he was mad as well, we were introduced, no doubt our parents thought it might benefit each of us. Visibly he was then travelling further along the psychiatric road than I was, with his decorated black cowboy hat, strutting, bouncy walk and witch doctor demeanour. His embrace of his inner world inspired me, for him this was not a temporary illusion but the true reality, to be treasured and valued and celebrated. He seemed to be the sane one, tuned into what was really going on, confident, creative and sure of himself, whereas I was not. He helped me along, unfazed by me but more drawn into his inner world than I was, he had decided who he was and got on with his life both in the physical and mystical worlds without conflict. He was being useful in both worlds, contributing in ways that I felt intuitively were helpful, without fully understanding what they were. He was creative, drawing, painting, playing guitar and sensitive underneath the cool, protective exterior, being caring towards me.

He had to accept Lithium injections as medication and his lifestyle firmly placed him in society as 'other'. He seemed to fully recognise the mystical world that I had been spending time in but my visits were brief by comparison. You could say he was a long term schizophrenic, or else a sensitive soul who the world had got to and that he was reacting to this by choosing to inhabit a safer mystical world instead. This world was good to share with someone, we hung out a number of times. I was trying to find my way back to some sort of reality that was more familiar to me than where I was currently at. Jamie helped me to better accept the place I was in now and feel more at peace with my situation.

We sat on a bench in the park one day and I talked to him of us both being 'Earth Healers', super powered mystics working to heal the damage done by humans to the Earth. He understood my passion and commitment to the environment but took different turns on the mystical path to me. It was a good, brief friendship, however despite our shared mental health issues we did not fully connect.

My recovery continued as I remained living downstairs at my parents' house in Chiswick. I started a bicycle repair business and bought and sold a few bikes too. I enjoyed being self-employed, working part-time and working at something I was good at. I acquired some more bicycle tools and regularly visited the cycle shop to buy more spare parts. What I did was high quality, slow work in the peace of my parents' back garden. It was good interacting with people, getting some local kids to learn about looking after their bikes and ensuring bicycle owners had safe, fully functioning bikes.

Chapter 85

I met an eccentric man as I was wandering about Chiswick, a tramp, an outcast, a wise man, with friendly eyes. I was walking near the house and saw him getting some wood out of a skip. He was trying to take a fair amount, so I helped him by working out how to load some onto a makeshift cart he had, and carried some myself. We walked and chatted our way back to his house, he apologised for taking me out of my way, I said I was very happy to help and that I enjoyed his company.

Dropping off the wood, we agreed to meet another time, we got on well, he had a most gentle nature about him.

On my first arranged visit I had a long chat with Bernard at his place, and invited him back for a cup of tea at my parents' house thereafter. This friendship saw me regularly visiting his house, and helping him sort out some of the extraordinary amount of belongings he had accumulated. The sorting generally consisted of working out how to stack and order things so as to create a little bit of space in which to fit more stuff. A challenging route through his hoard led to his kitchen and a couple of stools were placed amongst the chaos there. We sat, chatted and drank tea on a number of occasions, I found out that the small pile of rotting food he had was to encourage the fruit flies that lived there.

I ended up charging Bernard an hourly fee for helping him out at his house, which was one way of limiting my involvement in a potentially endless job, I wrote him receipts and worked eagerly, we also just met as friends and hung out sometimes. He told me about finding half a joint on the pavement that someone had left there for him one evening, then playing his guitar along to the radio until the early hours of the morning after smoking it. He felt totally connected with the radio show, he was an active participant, jamming, he said it was really going on, a great atmosphere, I wondered at how this isolated man had found such connection with people.

He had a navy background, having worked as a store man, and was a skilled engineer. He had some amazing welded figures that he had created as art, I wanted to buy one of them but he was not selling. My favourite was a humanoid figure walking along, the movement captured was so cool, the figure looked like some kind of total dude strutting his stuff confidently down the street. It seemed to me that he understood me very well and we shared a lot, I trusted this wise man and really felt at ease in his company.

He had an amazing relationship with birds, I think they loved him as much as he loved them. The 'runway' feeding station he used for them was the middle of Chiswick roundabout, a grassy area where not many humans trod. We scattered several loaves of bread for them one morning about quarter to nine, in the rush hour, with the motorway crossing above this triple lane roundabout with major junctions to all sides. It was not a quiet place but Bernard had found a peace there with nature. I was listening to the noise of the busy humans, around and above, in a hurry with their cars and their jobs and their hectic world.

I heard a psychic scream of distress, it was a female scream that stayed in my mind for about five seconds. I understood the scream, why this distress was there, it was an expression of pain and hurt about the unnatural, crazy rush that all these humans were in. Their combined efforts of leaving their houses, getting in their cars, sitting in traffic, becoming frustrated, polluting the world with fumes and anger. Their jobs that went against the course of nature, against the way of the world, making the Earth's wounds worse. This scream was the daily protest by a loving motherly spirit, asking why oh why must these humans repeat this terrible mistake day after day, and spoil the world.

Within the scream was the sound of surprise that humans had decided, today, again to follow this course of action. All humans had to do was to not go into work and do something else that was positive and helped to heal the world rather than wound it. There were so many things they could do that were harmonious with the way of the world, but yet, they kept on making the wrong choice. This pain and discordance with nature was very simple to stop and the world and civilisation could so easily change. The scream was urging everyone to stop the madness, this discordance with nature. I was glad to have heard this important, deep truth of our times, this spiritual expression, this protest against how so many millions of humans act daily.

Chapter 86

Bernard turned up at the house a number of times, once being invited in by my parents while I was out. I managed to get Dad involved helping Bernard tow a car from one place to another, the car was jammed full of stuff and Bernard seemed to live in it sometimes, I was glad my family was willing to help him out too. I decided to have a word with him about not dropping by randomly at my parents' house as they would not always be able to invite him in. Once we had a chat in the front garden, drinking tea, when he did not particularly wish to come in as it was a sun-filled day. The tree at the front was full of birds, more than I have ever seen in it before. Nature followed this special, gentle man with his large beard, dirty clothes and unwashed smell, a natural man.

He had tales of harassment by the council who had thrown away most of his things once, their total lack of sympathy and respect for his passion of collecting, hoarding. Bernard had a tale of fitting two machines together that just worked perfectly, without being designed to, but they became one, under his skilful hands. A story of working for someone and, even though he had become injured and bandaged, still feeling like he was expected to work, and telling his boss that the expectations were too much. A tale of a time working in a psychiatric hospital, outside in the garden, a patient was near a drain, dropping stones through the grate and listening to the plop as each one hit the water. Bernard told me of how he joined this person, also dropping stones, finding it a very satisfying activity to participate in, then feeling like he should get on with some work. I imagined Bernard, with his amazing mental strength and connection with nature, being someone who helped to shape the whole psychiatric hospital that he was in. He must have had a huge, but subtle influence on the workings, the human dynamics and regime there, due to his strong, subtle personality and being in harmony with the way of the world.

Bernard helped me to bridge the gap between the mental appreciation of environmentalism and the day-to-day practical application. He helped to make me more proactive and mindful, for example, questioning why I walked on the pavement on the right, aggressively walking against the polluting cars which I hated. He suggested that I could walk on the left pavement, with the flow of the traffic, with a more loving attitude and so have more of a positive effect upon that which I was trying to change, the traffic and pollution.

I remember him once questioning me after I had plucked a leaf off a tree. What had the tree done to me? Why did I harm it? When I later left the area, I said goodbye and thanked him, which he accepted humbly, he really helped me out at this difficult time, an outcast who understood. I took it as happy coincidence that Bernard shared the name of St. Bernard's psychiatric hospital, perhaps he was Saint Bernard.

Chapter 87

My mother told me that she had spoken about me with a friend of hers, Eileen, and that she was praying for me. I was struck by the generosity of her friend, that she would go out of her way for me like that. I was also struck by the simplicity of the action, the complete logical sense that it made. When faced with something that you feel powerless to change but wish to impact, it made sense to pray - what harm could it do? At least praying about someone is better than doing nothing, even if it is ineffective, at least it's trying, could it really do any harm? It made me feel cared about and somehow reassured that her God might be helping me out a bit, I certainly needed whatever help I could get, I later thanked Eileen for her help when I so needed it.

Jon was an old primary school friend who took some time hanging out with me, I remember listening to reggae music with him, trying to show him how Bob Marley had many meaningful things to say and how important they were. He had little interest in the music, and took the piss of how much I was into it, he moved his hand to the beat in a way that took on each beat. A take, take, take action, repeated, he was demonstrating to me how this was what reggae music was like to him, take, take, take, it was very similar to how I perceived myself too. I took, took from everyone and did not give much out, I felt I had nothing to give and needed to absorb the love and care from those around me in order to survive, 'take care, take care', sometimes repeated in my mind.

Jon had been the only friend with me all the way through both primary and secondary schools, we had drifted apart in our teenage years as I had discovered dope and made different friends to him. There was no undoing the hundreds of times we had been to each other's houses and many many hours of play we had experienced when we were younger. We had a friendship based on fun and doing stuff, he could see that I was bit paralysed, overthinking things and taking everything too seriously for my own good.

Once when we were walking along together he completely changed direction, I asked him what he was doing. 'I changed my mind', this conjured up thoughts and ideas in my head, that people could simply change their minds, switching from one course of action to another, and amazingly their mind would hold up to this change. So I tried it myself in some different ways and found it refreshing to just let go of everything that was in my mind, to empty it and fill it with a new direction or path. It helped me to be a bit less bogged down in my thoughts, to be less focused on dwelling upon something until I had worked it out. I was thinking about the meaning of sayings, a stitch in times saves nine and why rolling stones gather no moss, lots of them running through my head.

One day he came over and we went to the local park, armed with a tennis ball, I was in a lost world and physically stiff with stress, so going outside was a really good idea of Jon's. We played catch, the sort of catch that involves throwing the ball as far as you possibly can, over huge distances and with a lot of effort. We kept on managing to throw the ball straight to each other, then he started to encourage me to throw the ball to the side of him, as he did to me too. Having to move sideways quickly in order to catch the ball added a bit of extra challenge and fun. Jon encouraged me to throw it further and further to the side for him and he started to have to run quite far in order to catch it sometimes. I was more moderate in the speeds I could move at that day but Jon made up for it, the spectacle of him running as hard as he could to catch the ball was funny because his efforts were so lacking any deep and meaningful purpose, yet he was trying so hard.

I put lots of emotion into my throws, filling the ball with

important energy and just throwing it in the air. I was getting rid of some of the stress and seriousness that my mind was caught up in. I started to throw the ball impossibly far away for Jon to catch and still he tried, to both our amusements, I in turn started to find I could run for it too. In this way we shared something very special that day. It helped me release something that was stuck and holding me back. My trusted friend that I could throw my precious emotions to and know he would do his best to catch them. If the ball fell on the ground, it dissipated the huge amount of emotional energy onto the earth that I had imbued the ball with. It was okay because this was fun. Fun was something I was not having a great deal of at this time. Jon was unfazed by how mentally ill I came across as and did not doubt that the real me was there, underneath, just waiting to re-emerge. Having some fun was a very good way to help, he knew this intuitively, it was what we had always done when we were together.

Chapter 88

The laughs and fun that I needed did not come so much from my family environment, there were not so many laughs to be had at home, I could not remember when I had last seen anyone in my family laugh, still, the support offered from my sisters and parents was vital but I needed more than they had to give. In Hazel's house there was often laughter that would infect me and lift me, even if I did not laugh myself, it helped lift my spirits and brush some of the heaviness away that was such a dominant feature of my life. I found a certain solace at her place with her sisters and parents, all good at having a down to earth laugh, not taking themselves too seriously.

I continued to find support and solace with Hazel, she was amazing, we went out and about in cars, walks, camping and a sunny holiday with my family to Turkey where we smoked more than 200 cigarettes in a week. We smoked dope now and again throughout all our time together and enjoyed going out dancing on funk nights, playing whoops head card games, backgammon and having long nurturing cuddles.

Her family were very accommodating and I was often round there, soaking up the different atmosphere, needing their love. Hazel really helped me, and I gave a lot to her too, what I could, even though I was quite weird at times. She stood by and never lost sight of the fact that I was in a temporary situation of altered reality, helping me to affirm that belief too, even though she had never known me otherwise. Thankfully, I never lost sight of the belief that I was temporarily going through this journey, that things were not 'real', but strange for the time being. I thought it was like being at sea in a storm and waiting for the storm to blow itself out, then I would be okay, it just seemed like a long storm at times. 'Worse things happen at sea', at least I wasn't actually at sea with my mind in this disarray, having to cope with the wind and the waves and the sails and the forces of nature, all at the same time.

My psychosis was due to altered brain chemistry, just that little bit too much so that it couldn't quickly rebalance. It was getting there though and this was despite smoking every week or so, and having finished the medication course. I was healing well and being moderate in my smoking habits, not wanting to push the balance too far again. My diagnosis entirely fails to describe why I needed to smoke so much marijuana in India, why I pushed myself almost to oblivion. I believe it was because I could not cope with witnessing the suffering I saw in

India, nothing in my life so far had prepared me for it, I was traumatised. I was so deeply affected that I had to escape it and escape my feelings about that pain and suffering of so many innocents, post-traumatic stress, marijuana dulling the pain.

I met someone who said they cried for a week the first time they travelled to India. If I had been able to let my feelings out like that, they would not have needed dampening down with marijuana. I forced down my trauma by escaping it and dulling the pain in a stoned haze. Of course, it caught up with me, with the psychosis taking two years to unravel, until I felt relatively stable again, a gradual adjustment to the new me.

Chapter 89

I got into the origins of written language a bit, and wanted to know more about Sanskrit, which I believed to be the original one. There were those ancient carvings at the Tiger Temple that seemed to indicate an advanced aspect to the old civilisation, perhaps knowing teleport secrets, revealed through the magic of their language. I thought that modern English had lost some vital energies along its evolutionary pathway. So tracing back the language could ensure the initial vitality was captured. The first written words may have been the most important concepts to ancient human civilisations and so carry great meaning.

It was a complicated and slow thing to study at my local library, the internet barely existed. I became sidetracked by a book that was a transcript of a very deep philosophical conversation by some sort of wise Guru, a clever Indian man, unlocking the secrets of life but not part of a cult or religion, just facts really. It was good to find that so locally, I took it as I sign that I should read it, having found it as I browsed through the shelves.

There were many signs guiding me, all I had to do was look, often messages on the number plates of cars meant something individual and special to me, I found a very high quality size 10 Britool spanner in the road, which was perfect for bicycle maintenance and better than anything I had, another sign. I was being guided and communicated with by billboard adverts, TV and films, and sometimes the radio would play something that was just for me, for my benefit, me alone. So much help was being poured out to me, it made me feel supported and loved by civilisation and invoked a sense of responsibility that I needed to get myself better and help the world again, as it was helping me.

Chapter 90

I had experience of making pots on the wheel at a place in Richmond and got a technician job where I loaded a kiln, mixed glazes, fired pots, recycled used clay and pottered around, tidying. I would come when there were no classes to do my work, once chatting with a teacher there tidying up after a lesson who asked me to get her some hash, which I did. It was a peaceful job, in a creative place in the quiet atmosphere, part-time and minimal stress.

I could often see connections between the work that was being made and myself, some pieces were a tribute to me as a thank you for my work there. Some students were influenced by me into making something arty that I could then relate to myself, like I was a mystical influence helping people to shape pots, which was helping them along their own paths. People were following me and learning, I was helping them by firing their pots.

My advanced path of spiritual consciousness was, through these creations, being brought into being on a different level, reaching more people. There was a bit of a spiritual revolution happening through these creations being made with the influence from me. The spiritual energies were being manifested and solidified into pieces of work. The physical pieces meant concepts could be seen and understood on a subtle level, by everyone who saw them and worked with them, bringing down to earth this knowledge, from the spiritual heights from where it came, it was all related to helping society to go more with the way of the world.

The feeling of my supreme influence entirely changed at some point, a new spiritual influence arrived, affecting all the works being created by the students, I had no problem accepting this alternative influence, perhaps a new teacher, or possibly student, had taken over from me spiritually leading the students ever onwards. It meant that all that needed to be manifested that related to my spiritual knowledge had been created, that this spiritual knowledge had now been imbued in works of art, communicating this deep and important knowledge to other humans.

One day I visited with Hazel, she encouraged me to sit at the wheel to be creative, releasing some of my pent up energies, but I did not have the inspiration or motivation to make anything, feeling frozen, managing only just to perform the basic technician duties I had to fulfil to keep pace with the needs of the workshop and the creations I carefully fired. I dropped Hazel at her college then hit a car on my way home, no injuries, just the result of my spaced out driving. I continued to drive my Mum's car around London, managing to bend a door back on a concrete bollard after I had reversed, forgetting it was still open.

Chapter 91

There was a part of me that had known I was asking for trouble when I first said hi to them, and decided to branch off the High Street. I think I saw that they needed help in some way, so I made myself available to them and ended up exchanging money for environmental wisdom.

I was taking a long walk back home one evening, about eleven pm when I passed two dodgy looking guys on Chiswick High Street and said hello to them. Shortly after, I turned off, cutting through a quiet street, I had a feeling of uncertainty about my decision to turn off the High Street, just after speaking to these two lads. It was dark, they came up to me and I found they were not very friendly. After asking me for my my pin number, in a dark area round the corner from the bank, one went to an ATM where they took the day's cash limit. They then took me to a grassy area near the tube line tracks and continued to verbally threaten me, pressed a small knife against my neck, and took out a tiny gun which they sometimes held against the side of my head, or sometimes in my mouth. I knew these guys were all talk and no action, they waited with me in the shadowed part of the grassy area until midnight and then one of them went to take the next day's daily limit from my account.

While the other one was left with me, I gave him a lecture on the importance of recycling, he was slightly calmer than the first guy who soon returned. Having given them my house keys and told them my correct address, I was asked to climb over the fence and run along the railway line while they made their escape. The run along the tracks was a great relief to me, using up my overcharged adrenaline. I got home and then went to report the mugging with my Dad at the local police station. He quickly and needlessly changed the locks on the front and back doors, I knew they would not remember the address but I had not wished to lie to them when they had asked. They were crackheads, desperate for the next hit, thankfully they had not done me any physical harm and I had not been truly scared of them, I felt sorry for them.

Before long, a supportive councillor volunteer person came to see me, to help me to get over the trauma of the mugging. We had a short chat, I didn't really connect with him and didn't feel significantly traumatised, so I thanked him for his efforts and chose not to see him again. The next official step was the identity parade where I asked everyone to say 'lovely sunny day', there was no doubt that two of the guys in line were the exact two that had robbed me. I was amazed that the police had tracked them both down so quickly and brought them into custody. It turned out they had robbed another young man just a few days later, he had his clothes taken which he later found in a dustbin. We chatted together in court, he seemed a really nice, gentle person.

Somehow, I guess it was due to the gun, or the two incidents in such a short space of time, the case was heard at the Old Bailey High Court in central London, my mother and a friend of hers came and sat in the gallery. One of the lads spoke to me in the foyer outside of the courtroom, demanding that I 'come here', I was given advice by my friendly police escort to 'just ignore him'. Afterwards, I was given a copy of my statement that I had originally given to the police because I asked for it, and very confidently read it out in court. The cross examination was along the lines of 'could I be sure it was them because it was dark', I was absolutely sure that it was them standing right there, and I made that very clear, confidently testifying.

I decided to go home once I had testified, as I was not needed again. Mum said the trial went on for several days, with each and every member of the young men's families swearing blind that the lads had been elsewhere, doing other things. They each got five-year sentences and would likely be out in three, I still felt sorry for them, sorry that putting them in prison was the pathetic best that the society I lived in had to offer, which really was not going to help with the underlying reasons for them being crackheads. I was not in a position to provide an alternative option so had little chance but to go along with this plan.

The bank paid me back and a small mention was made in the local paper. I was shaken by everything that had happened with this incident but quickly processed it and moved onwards, a sign that I was so much stronger mentally, probably stronger than I had been before. No doubt it was a relief to those close to me that I was okay and not sliding back into another intense psychotic episode.

Chapter 92

My friend Tam asked me to come along to help a guy deliver a barge, we helped cast off from the shore and then spent the voyage relaxing on the deck in the sun leisurely cruising the Thames. At one point, on the deck, I was in the centre of a powerful Mandala, the boat was in the centre of the river and I was here, with my mathematically clever friend with the people of London surrounding us on all sides. I experienced a Godly feeling of power and a desire to change the world for the better, using this power. I was involved with a symmetrical incantation that was positively affecting everyone around me, on the shore, in nearby buildings and on boats, I was doing some important, powerful work.

Eventually we came into dock at the end of the voyage and were standing by ready, approaching the dock when the guy suddenly decided to turn sharply to one side, without warning, to take a slightly shorter route straight to the dock. The barge slowly ground to a halt, it had hit something underneath and was stuck, off the marked route into the dock lay these dangers for the captain. I was shaken by the action and the thought of possible damage. I believed that it was me who had caused this to happen. Once it was confirmed that the barge was stuck, there was nothing more that Tam and I could do, we were given a lift to the shore and money for a taxi back home.

I said to Tam that it was all my fault and he said that it was the guy's fault who was steering the barge and that he was a bit strange. I found this reassuring and tried to convince myself that it really was his fault. However, I knew that the super strong mystical powers I was caught up in that day had been capable of just about anything. I tried to reassure myself that the man had made the sudden decision to steer to the side, independent of me. He had not trusted in the main, safe path ahead of him to the dock. He had suddenly reached the end of his patience with this longer, slower route and taken a rash shortcut, this was a choice he had made.

I had put pressure on him by giving him the huge responsibility of carrying a Godly person - myself, working to change the world, sending out the Mandala communications and influences all around me that day on his boat. Every small decision he made had to be the right one as this journey was influencing so many people along the way, he may have wanted the journey to come to an end as soon as possible because of the pressure of the huge responsibility thrust on him by myself. He cracked just near the end, and that was his fault, not mine, I tried not to worry too much about my certain influence behind this crash.

A photo taken later showed the bows of the barge lifted into the air revealing a wooden beam, part of the dock structure that the barge had hit. The position of the barge had become more dramatic as the tide had gone out and then it had floated free again as the tide rose, safely getting to its destination undamaged but late. I was glad about that and mindful of the lesson to be learned from this man's impulsive actions.

I watched a documentary about a tribe of people who lived near the equator in South America, they were called the Kogi. They were very wise and chose not to embrace technology in their villages but had a beautiful, spiritual life, nine physical worlds, nine spiritual, all coexisting and honoured by the Kogi in all aspects of their daily lives. People had set roles in the village, some were wise leaders who had a long induction in childhood, others were like police, enforcing the orders, the rest were general helpers. When people were ill they went into separate, quiet houses and some members of the tribe looked after them.

The programme really inspired me, these people believed they were helping to keep the balance of spiritual energy over the whole world in harmony. Their message was a request to stop stealing from the special graves of their ancestors, which helped keep the global spiritual balance and stop taking so many resources from the Earth, instead live in harmony with the world in physical and spiritual harmony with it. I loved the way they had everything in life so worked out and lived an ideal life, surrounded by nature, away from civilization, through choice. I was inspired, bought their book and tried to apply their logic to the world around me, it worked to some extent, and to some extent London was a different, incompatible place. Hazel patiently listened to me telling her all about it.

Another time I visited a trendy London cinema with Tam, he had invited me to see Akira which had recently come out and I knew nothing about. I identified very strongly with the lead male and thought of his friends and their support in the film being like the supportive friends of mine. It was a poignant film to see at this time, as it totally applied to and related to me, dramatising a man's struggle with his own huge mental powers, barely controlling them, having great influence all around him.

I later watched Blue Velvet with my parents at a local cinema, the strange film washed over me, creating a minor disturbance, which seeped away, the song stuck in my head a long time afterwards.

Chapter 93

I had quite a bit of discussion with Betty and my parents about which university to go to, I decided on Kent at Canterbury to study Chemistry with Environmental Science. Compared with others such as Lancaster, which I visited and loved, Kent university was near to London and my parents in case I was not well, a safer choice. I was going to be an Industrial Chemist working right in the heart of that which was harming the environment to try to turn things around, changing things from within, helping to make the whole industry that bit more environmentally friendly. The huge scale of environmental damage made by industry seemed to me number one priority for me to do something about, utilising my chemistry skills.

Before university I went to Jersey where my aunt lived with my sister Zoe, we took a guitar and I learned to play a positive, upbeat blues riff. In some way this represented my acceptance of experiencing the blues and having now the ability to find positivity in my day to day life, not letting the blues get me down. Strange things were still were happening to me, mostly in my head, but I could get on with life better. Zoe was trying to help me, my aunt did too, it was a fairly mellow time, nice to get away from the suffocation of the millions surrounding me in London.

Both my sisters tried, and helped in their own way to steer me in the right direction, as of course did my parents and friends, all doing what they could, helping to navigate me through the storm at sea that I was in, far out from the safety of land where they stood, as I weathered the storm in my lonesome boat.

I bought a VW Polo for two hundred quid and loved it, four gears and a large boot space that just fitted a potters wheel with the seats down, I took one to university which was good therapy the few times I used it.

One afternoon at university towards the beginning I was feeling pretty disturbed and called Hazel, I drove over to her place in London, and received some much needed nurturing from her. I left at midnight, returning to the usual routine at university the following day. Hazel soon after decided to part company with me, an inevitable result of us living in Kent and London, I reluctantly agreed.

I was not long in embracing and utilising the new and numerous opportunities available at university. I made friends with artists, jugglers, oddballs, performers, musicians and two people on the Chemistry course. I had a fun time, with the social life eclipsing the intricacies of Chemistry that I was meant to be there for. I found I was more focused on people and a social life, playing in a band, girlfriends, parties, alcohol and drugs, adventures in the countryside and by the sea.

I was still a bit weird, but integrating, independent and enjoying life, increasingly extroverted. I found that the student union post for the environment was vacant, I had half an hour to collect twelve nominations, I did this from random students whom I stopped and asked to sign the form. I learned about the workings of the student union, had a bit of positive influence on the environment and went about my duties as an executive officer of the student union in a most laid-back manner.

I met a woman I felt a strong psychic connection with at a party, Sacha, and we had an amazing, intense, wild, passionate relationship. We were both based by the sea, I was living Whitstable and she was a walk along the shore to Seasalter. We picked and ate magic mushrooms on a trip to Dartmoor and during the trip we discussed my future, and I realised that it was really important that I did what made me happy, and prioritise that. I had been doing this course with a view to helping the world and felt I had the responsibility to continue to do so for the greater good, whether or not I enjoyed it. I did not know what I wanted to do but realised that another two years of this course was not what I wanted. On returning back from my break I left the course feeling a tremendous sense of relief that I had prioritised what I needed for me, even if that meant an uncertain future.

Sacha and I split up after a few months, I performed in a play at university, did some odd jobs, cleaned at Tesco, moved house to where a twenty two year old cat lived, signed on the dole for a bit, then after visiting London for Christmas, I decided there was not much more for me back in Kent, so returned to my parents again.

Chapter 94

I found a project that needed volunteers to survey Harbour Porpoise in Shetland where they are called Neesick, the local word referring to the sound they make on a calm quiet sea as they swim to the surface to breathe out and in. I shared an ageing camper van with a very well educated bloke who smoked a lot of dope, and got to meet all sorts of environmental types, spending many hours surveying the sea, enjoying the peaceful pace of the volunteer work. I had no desire to smoke dope and did not, instead I left the project after a couple of months.

I contacted a friend of my uncle's and through her contacted her boyfriend Jim, I saw him at his house and asked if I could leave my rucksack and bicycle at his while I looked for somewhere to live. 'You can live here if you like' he said and I did so for the next nine months, Shetland helped to heal me, body and soul.

I lived in a croft house, rode a 50cc moped, then a 125cc motorbike, then a 350cc, did gardening work, made long-lasting friends. I was still odd, but at peace within, often silent, but alert and switched on, I went years without smoking a joint. I returned to London now and again, staying at my parents'. The croft house I had moved to was very basic, off the road, through fields, no track or electricity and no roof to the kitchen extension where the tap was. It was a home, I was free and loved renovating it. My cousin came and helped for a couple of weeks and I got local help too, it was still not a great place to be in the extreme winds of winter and so I either migrated south to London or stayed again with Jim through the wild ,wild dark Shetland winters.

On one winter migration, I moved to a therapeutic community in Dorset, living there and giving my time to help the place along. I made many friends there and met a very disturbed woman whom I decided to move in with in Brighton as her informal carer, we got on well as friends. It was sometimes extremely intense but I helped her and learned a lot from her. After a month or two I moved out, needing my space, I started working as a labourer in a pottery. I continued to see her often at her flat, and visited her in the psychiatric hospital when she was admitted there. I maintained our friendship from a distance when I returned to Shetland again.

During another southerly migration, I got another job, through Tam's dad again, and set to working on boats near Hammersmith Bridge. It was idyllic, cycling to work along the river and being out on a pier all day, driving a speedboat and painting boats and doing unskilled work on them. One of the highlights was going into central London on a speedboat during a tube strike, so few people using the river, I went flat out as much as I dared.

As the tide went down one day a body was revealed on the shore opposite, I looked at it a long time as it was my first corpse. The river police came and collected it, saying they get suicides every week, I thought he was a recent immigrant falling on hard times in the city and deciding to end his life, his clothes were cheap and he looked poor.

The pier led to another job, of doing up a house, a hard few months labouring with a guy who did everything in the greatest hurry with no time taken for the quality of work, it was how I was expected to work as well. I adjusted and kept pace with him, on one memorable afternoon on the scaffolding, managing to single handedly paint the entire of the front of the house with watered down masonry paint. Reau worked nearby and somehow we met up, briefly rekindling our flame, doing something to resolve the fractured way that I had split up with her.

I stayed in Shetland for a number of years and was deeply healed by the experience, meeting amazing people in this tranquil place, wild and free. This peace, surrounded by nature, far away from London, this simple life, Shetland is where I healed my wounds and strengthened my soul.

I read a lot, including the Bible and found I could relate to it deeply, but struggled to relate to any sort of church, trying out many. I gained some support from various lovely church goes I met and found that there was a religious viewpoint to many of my experiences which I related to. I gradually realised that I preferred an individual, private and personal spiritual life, without the interference of organised religion. I was surprised each time I met others with the same outlook, thinking I might be almost the only one.

I returned to India in 1996 doing voluntary work interspersed with backpacking travelling whenever I needed a break from the emotional stresses of caring for those in such dire need. I worked with street kids in Bombay (Mumbai), orphans in Tamil Nadu and with the nuns in a Home For The Destitute And Dying in Calcutta. I empathised with peoples' suffering but handled it well by doing something about it.

The barriers of backpacker tourist observing those in need were broken down, I got to know the people I was helping a bit and had fun with them too, I also connected with other volunteers. I felt part of a larger, positive effort that was making a difference and that was something vital that I contributed to. By doing this, I did not dwell on the depth and enormity of suffering, that was still very much there, I did not feel guilty about my own privileged life. Because, by doing something about it on the front line, immersed in the moment, fully engaged in helping to the best of my ability I was doing all I could to assist. I did become worn out, so nurtured myself by going to Goa, the Himalayas, staying in an Indian village, staying next to the sea, but just for a couple of weeks, then back to it again.

I did smoke marijuana, but recreationally, not recklessly, only in peaceful places when I was having a break from volunteer work. I did not wish to revisit previous places, because that was then and this was a new experience, moving forward in life, a changed person. I managed nearly six months, returning safe and sound. I learned that whatever little I could do, that little bit helped the people who needed so much, even if it was just for that day or that hour, it is far better to do something than nothing. I made a difference, however small, and that was something vitally important to those I helped. These experiences led me towards full time care work in the UK afterwards.

I reunited some five years after university with Sacha, after writing to her, pouring out my heart and not expecting a reply. She bravely moved up with me from Bristol to Shetland, we were in love. I so enjoyed doing care work that after a few years, I decided to do my Mental Health Nursing qualification. I had a daughter with Sacha in

Shetland and we all moved to Dumfries and Galloway for me to attend the nursing college there.

I was first rejected by the college because I had honestly answered the questions about the mental health experiences I had experienced which were, at that time, ten years in the past. My GP helped by explaining to them that I had recovered and that I was no longer mentally ill or in danger of becoming so, this made the college change their mind. As a student nurse, I was extremely careful about telling people about my past experiences in case I was again rejected by the perversely biased system I had chosen to join.

Sacha and I lived together for seventeen years and had two children. We helped each other grow into ourselves and realise our potential until we no longer needed each other and went our separate ways again.

I found that help is harder to receive than to give, being ill made me realise that the vast majority of people are really helpful and kind.

I am still nursing. I think I will be helping those in need in one way or another for the rest of my life as I have not found anything more compelling, fulfilling or enjoyable to do.

An environmentally helpful urge   1993

Environmental helping urge,
What can I do now?
Write a protest letter,
Makes me feel better.
Plant a tree?
I can't, I haven't got any.
I could always read about,
How life on earth is dying out.
I'll make a cup of tea,
To have, reading my book,
Hang on,
I'm still doing something wrong.

Than electricity is nuclear,
And that cooker makes CO2,
A greenhouse affecter and,
Nuclear power plant selector.

If I just sit here,
In the dark here,
Just breathing slowly air,
Brushing my long hair.

I begin to relax,
My body goes slack,
And I do nothing,
nothing,
nothing.

Later on, I, from that awake,
I've saved my environment,
And that's great.

<u>Some notes I made throughout the years I mulled over this book</u>

I went to India in 1990.

1992 to 1996

I have decided to go to the effort of writing this book, as I started compiling a little bit of what had happened and then my notes grew and grew, there was a book's worth of material to be expressed, and so I chose to write it, mostly for my peace of mind. I have never written a book before but the experiences I went through while travelling in India were so profound that I wanted to share them with others. I feel that as there are a lot of people going to India on a budget travel basis in the way that I did, this might act as some sort of guide and companionship in the undertaking of the difficult trip. The book has taken years to write, with long periods of neglect, but it has been mostly enjoyable to get it all out of my system before I go back to India again (did so in 1996). However, many of the mind opening, spiritual experiences might have happened anywhere. I have decided to return to India in order to set some things within myself at rest and because I love the place and feel deep and strong connections with many people out there. Perhaps as I travel more widely I might feel like that wherever I go.

2001

Finally I feel ready to let this book loose and to take the flack that might come from that decision. I am now studying to be a mental health nurse and still sometimes have a wee smoke here in Scotland.

2002

I have just got to go through it all and get someone to look it over and then get it published.

2003

Gave the book to an editor friend to read who said it had good material and was not just a personal account, she gave me some suggestions for total restructuring to make it a book that captured the present day and the reflective account. I was not keen on the restructuring but I was pleased it had good material in it and was interesting to read.

2015

Typed out my original written account of the beginning of the trip and carefully joined together the overlapping written and typed parts of the book together, giving preference to the original written version.

2016

Read through the book and tweaked it to ensure a better flow without changing content

2018 – Some 29 years after the trip.

During some recent time in between jobs I added all the bits I had missed out, deleted little bits and ensured a smoother flow. I found that many of the bits I needed to add were the most difficult and challenging times that this book covers. I found it surprisingly therapeutic to return to these memories and was surprised at the level of detail that I was still able to recall for so many of the events. I also found that I had a surprisingly huge number of hours more work to give to the book. I got the assistance of a proofreader to smooth out my erratic flow with some collaborative creative editing.

2019 – Final tweaks and publish. A huge project all in all with many hundreds of hours of writing and reflection. 251 pages.

I have written this book because it kept asking to be written and would not stop reminding me, even when I ignored it for a decade. Its been good therapy to finish this, if others enjoy it and get something from it too, then I see that as a bonus.

Aaron X

Printed in Great Britain
by Amazon